Praise for Who Stole My Spandex?

"Marcia Kester Doyle writes with supreme wit. She's brutally honest, blissfully funny, and an absolute blast to read."

—AK Turner, New York Times bestselling author of *This Little Piggy Went to the Liquor Store* and *Hair of the Corn Dog*

* * *

"Curl up with a glass of wine, a copy of *Who Stole My Spandex?* and let the giggling begin. (Disclaimer: I cannot, however, be held responsible if a jet stream of wine shoots out of your nose when your giggles turn into full-fledged guffaws. Read responsibly.)

—Leighann Lord, stand-up comedian and author of *Dict Jokes: Alternate Definitions for Words You've Probably Never Heard of But Will Definitely Never Forget*

* * *

"This book is hilarious and heartwarming. You will laugh. You will cry. And you won't want it to end. Marcia is able to take even the most ordinary life situation and make it laugh-out-loud funny. Take a moment to treat yourself with the gift of laughter. Hide in the bathroom if you have to, but every midlife woman should read this book!"

—Vikki Clafin, author of *Shake, Rattle & Roll With It*

"Marcia Kester Doyle describes everyday occurrences and middle-age realities with a slam-dunk of wit and humanity. The stories are varied and offer entertaining descriptions of topics not often thought of as funny: colonoscopies, menopause, teenagers, aging, and empty nests, just to name a few. Warning: will cause bursts of laughter at the beach and poolside."

—Kimberly J. Dalferes, author of *Magic Fishing Panties* and *I Was in Love With a Short Man Once*

* * *

"No matter what life has dished up for her, Marcia Kester Doyle has an uncanny gift for seeing and sharing the humor or beauty in every situation. … I'm awed by her ability to make me both laugh and cry in the same book. Hold all my calls, I'm meeting Marcia for take-out from the Burger Barn."

—Leslie Marinelli, CEO of In The Powder Room and editor and co-author of the bestselling women's humor anthology, *You Have Lipstick On Your Teeth*

* * *

"Marcia Kester Doyle's book *Who Stole my Spandex?* is the gift to myself that keeps on giving. I read it once, and then read it again and laughed every time! It's 100 percent relatable for anyone going through 'the change,' and 100 percent hysterical."

—Tracy Beckerman, syndicated humor columnist and author of *Lost In Suburbia*

"*Who Stole My Spandex?* is required reading for anyone who enjoys laughter at any age. Marcia Kester Doyle has the ability to turn a seemingly everyday event, mishap, or unexpected 'issue' into a cause for celebration and high amusement. She writes so honestly and entertainingly about her life and loves, channeling Erma Bombeck with humor, verve, warmth, and hard-won wisdom!"

—Jenny Isenman, humorist behind TheSuburbanJungle.com and Jenny From the Blog, on-air host for NBC, and writer at the Huffington Post, Yahoo! Shine, and The Stir

* * *

"With each new chapter of *Who Stole My Spandex?*, I laughed until I cried, and that was amazing. Marcia swept me away with her incredible ability to find the joy in even the most trying times. She may be the only person I know who could leave me wishing to survive a natural disaster because, like with everything else in her life, she does it with a beautiful balance of humor and grace!"

—Carolyn Coppola, author of *Minivans Meltdowns & Merlot*

* * *

"This book kept my sides splitting for days. If you are middle-aged or approaching middle age, I think this is the book to laugh down all the trials and tribulations that come with this 'wondrous' time in our lives."

—Donna Cavanagh, founder of HumorOutcasts.com

"It's difficult to write humor, but Marcia Kester Doyle does it in grand style. This book is easy to read, provokes needed laughter, and makes you want to get together with Marcia for a road trip. It could be like Thelma and Louise, but without the messy driving-over-the-cliff scene. I look forward to more books from this author."

—Elaine Ambrose, syndicated blogger and author of 10 books, including *Menopause Sucks* and *Midlife Cabernet*

* * *

"A comical glimpse at everything related to marriage, motherhood and middle age. Marcia's brand of humor had me laughing the entire time. I particularly enjoyed her humorous insight on raising a family and all the calamities that ensue. A delightful read!"

—Stacey Gustafson, author of *Are You Kidding Me?*

Who Stole My Spandex?
Life in the Hot Flash Lane

By Marcia Kester Doyle

Mill Park Publishing
www.MillParkPublishing.com

Edited by Sarah del Rio (sarahdelrio@gmail.com)
Cover Design by Michelle Fairbanks/Fresh Design

MarciaKesterDoyle.com
@MenoMother

The following chapters were originally published on the website "In the Powder Room" (http://inthepowderroom.com/) and are reprinted in part or whole (some titles changed) with permission: "Nine Signs You Might Be a MILF" (Jan. 2014), "The Truth About Aging" (Dec. 2013), "Livin' Large in Zumba Land" (originally published under the title "I Wanna Get Physical—With Mexican Food," Nov. 2013), "Aviation Traumatization" (originally published under the title "The Reason I'm Not In The Mile High Club," Nov. 2013), "Gobble Be Gone" (Nov. 2013), "Not In My Back Yard" (originally published under the title "The Neighbors From Hell," Jan. 2014), "In-Laws From Hell" (Jan. 2014), "Twelve Reasons Why She's Your Best Friend" (Nov. 2013), "Ladies' Restroom Etiquette 101" (Nov. 2013), "Six Good Things About Raising Teenage Boys" (Jul. 2013), and "Six Good Things About Raising Teenage Girls" (Jul. 2013).

Previously published as *Who Stole My Spandex? Midlife Musings From A Middle-Aged MILF*, Blue Lobster Book Co., 2014

Print ISBN 978-0-9883-9806-1
EPUB ISBN 978-0-9883-9808-5
Library of Congress Control Number: 2015918033

To Mac, for never letting me go a day without
laughter, and for helping me to see the
extraordinary in the ordinary.

In loving memory of my father, Stewart R. Kester,
and my sweet sister, Cherie.

Table of Contents

Introduction

I COME FROM A GENERATION of shoulder pads, mullets, and the incredible synthetic fabric known as spandex. While Cyndi Lauper was busy convincing the world that "Girls Just Want to Have Fun," I was combing the sales racks at Sears for anything containing 20 percent or more of this magical miracle material. The industrious little fabric with the futuristic name was the answer to the prayers of every fast-food-lovin' Baby Boomer who couldn't afford a plastic surgeon.

Throughout the years, spandex has kept my derriere lifted, my tummy tucked, and my "gals" facing north (even after they started to head in the opposite direction). It has given me the confidence to strut my stuff even when I look more like a microwave-inflated marshmallow than a sexy, middle-aged mama. It's all in the attitude. While others whine about the passing of time, I embrace it—after all, what better age to let the freak flag fly?

I'm a caffeine-addicted and somewhat accident-prone wife, mother, and firm believer that Nutella is proof that God loves us. You'll learn more about me as you get further into this book, where you'll find a collection of stories that will make you want to chug a martini and laugh so hard your spandex splits.

As for my family members, our lives together have always been, and continue to be, a delightful mosaic of love and laughter. We dream of inventing robotic beer butlers and tequila-laced ice packs, and our dinner conversations often revolve around topics such as toenail farms, dog puke, and "doodie." We love a good food fight, and are known for wearing cat masks around the fire pit on a cold winter's night. We're not ashamed of our Flintstone-era minivan, or the fact that our home could easily be mistaken for a petting zoo. Hey, even wayward rodents and flatulent pugs need a place to call home!

As I open my heart and bare my soul, some of my stories may have you reaching for the Kleenex—but in general, you'll find that my family prefers to look at the funny side of life. The minute things get too heavy, someone will break out into a Journey song—or announce that their bowels are about to erupt like Mount St. Helens. This, my friends, is life in the Nut House.

Welcome to my home!

One Size Fits None

I HATE SHOPPING for clothes, which explains why I've never been accused of being a fashionista. It also explains why my daughters always call to ask what I'm wearing before bringing their friends over to the house.

After birthing four babies by C-section, I now find shopping for clothes less enticing than a root canal. I might enjoy it more if I was twenty-five pounds lighter. Shopping just isn't as fun when I have to head straight for the Woman's Plus department, where everything comes in black, white, or shower-curtain pattern.

My husband often accompanies me during my clothes-hunting expeditions, usually because he is: a) bored with all five hundred cable channels, b) in need of replenishing his tube sock collection, or c) wanting to make sure I don't spend all my cash on animal-print house dresses and takeout from Burger Barn. He parks his butt on a sofa outside the changing rooms and plays with his phone while I'm pondering the age-old question of zippers versus control-top panels.

I try to be frugal while I shop, but the problem with the clearance section is that there are only two clothing sizes left on the rack by the time I get there: hummingbird and mastodon. It's always a challenge to find an outfit that doesn't leave me looking like the exploding dough from a tube of Pillsbury crescent rolls.

It's the same adventure every time I go shopping. I shoot past the regular lingerie (like I'll ever be able to squeeze myself into a hot fuchsia number the size of a rubber band) to the "Full Figure" aisle, where the bras hang like double-boulder slingshots. Then I whiz past the shoe section, jewelry department, and all those adorable maternity outfits. I think, "Oh, look at the cute, faux-denim stretch pants designed to hide a pregnancy bump!" before self-consciously rubbing my stomach. Nope, no baby in there—just the jelly roll the last kid left behind.

Once I'm able to find a dress that doesn't resemble a large paint tarp, I grab a few more items (twelve, actually, because I have no idea what the size *du jour* is going to be—I need a sampler platter of three different sizes for each outfit). I then head for the dreaded dressing room with an armload of clothes that will most likely end up back on the rack. It's always at this moment that I wish I lived in the 1500s, where everyone bought one-size-fits-all clothing from Dirty Smocks "R" Us, and dressed by dim candlelight to mask the effects of a stout-and-potato diet.

I'm wary of stepping into dressing rooms because I know there are some shoppers who use these cubicles for more than just trying on clothes. I know this because several of my children have worked in major department stores over the years, and they've shared a few nightmare tales that have scarred me for life. Department stores should consider posting helpful signs to keep paranoid people like me from worrying about stepping into DNA samples left by the previous occupants. The signs could flash messages like "FECAL-FREE ZONE!" or "MOTEL 6 IS DOWN THE STREET ... THEY'LL LEAVE A LIGHT ON FOR YOU!"

Wishing to God for a shot of liquid courage before I enter the "chamber of truth," I stall by the clearance rack for a few more minutes, until a skinny, perky salesclerk approaches me. She asks if I'm ready to try on my new clothes, and her chipper tone sets my teeth on edge. Can't she see I'm breaking into a sweat over the fact that my actual dress size is about to be revealed?

I'm ushered into a mirrored cubicle the size of Thumbelina's closet, and told to "have fun" while trying on the clothes. Have fun? The only way that would ever happen is if the dressing room included a well-stocked mini fridge. No, this is where the true horror begins. I shimmy out of my old, comfortable clothes and cringe as I view myself in panoramic funhouse mirrors that display my front, back, and sides. I'm immediately reminded of a peeled potato.

Concluding that the department store must have gotten a really good deal on mirrors from a traveling circus, I weed through my pile of clothing. One floral-print dress is reminiscent of something my grandmother wore in 1939. An orange blouse makes me look like an Oompa Loompa. An ill-fitting pair of jeans causes my flesh to ooze out over the waistband like Play-Doh. To make matters worse, I'm having to struggle into all of this torturous clothing under unflattering fluorescent lights that expose every fold, flap, bulge, and scar bestowed upon my body by childbirth and years of yo-yo dieting.

I decide on a few items of clothing that promise to lift, tuck, flatten, and flatter the body, and I notice that everything I've chosen is: a) made of NASA-approved spandex and b) one shade—black. So what if I end up with a bag of clothing resembling a mortician's closet?

I approach the checkout counter, and it never fails—there's always an angry woman ahead of me shouldering three returns and a missing receipt. To top it all off, she was clearly once the president of her high school debate team. My eye starts twitching as she engages in refund warfare with the young girl behind the cash register. Obviously neither one of these women knows that I'm already two hours late to walk a dog known for his daily bouts of IBS.

Once home, I face the daunting task of cleaning out old clothes to make room for the new. I'm a firm believer in recycling, and have found some creative ways to repurpose my granny panties with a needle and thread. With a garbage bag full of threadbare underpants and a few quick stitches, I can make an outdoor patio umbrella, a tent for camping trips, or an heirloom quilt for the grandkids.

I try the new clothes on again in the privacy of my own bedroom, but they don't look as good as they did in the dressing room. This just confirms what I've believed all along—that department store mirrors are designed to make every woman appear as shapely as an hour glass. When I look in my own mirror at home, all I see is a potato dressed up in a shower curtain. A black shower curtain.

Chances are good that I'll be returning all of my one-size-fits-none clothing to the mall—but only after a quick stop at the Burger Barn.

Hands off My Egg Roll!

NOT LONG AGO, while on a dogged and determined quest to find the perfect anniversary card, I decided to visit a gift shop at the nearby mall. Once inside, I immediately came upon a row of cutesy, but annoying, plaques that had obviously been designed to cheer up depressed friends and stressed-out coworkers.

One plaque in particular caught my attention, if only because I'd seen it dozens of times before—at the hair salon, the dentist's office, even in the checkout line at the local bakery. It's a popular sign designed to soothe irate customers, and it reads: "Don't Sweat the Small Stuff." The cheerful sentiment is often accompanied by a frazzled-looking female with curlers in her hair, or a dog with pathetic eyes and an expression that seems to say, "Please remove the pooping hamster that little Johnny left on my head. Please."

In addition to being a Hallmark cliché, the phrase "Don't Sweat the Small Stuff" also moonlights as a comforting thing to say when trying to calm or reassure folks in casual conversation. It works well on a lot of people—hence its popularity—but it doesn't work on me. I snub the logic of "Don't Sweat the Small Stuff" because there are some things in this world that I just *love* to hate.

For example:

Misplaced reading glasses. This gets particularly annoying when I can't read the telephone number on my cell phone, or when

I'm in a dimly lit restaurant and unable to read the menu. "Does this say crab or squab?"

When my children "borrow" my things. These items can range anywhere from scissors and pens to leftover Chinese food. I'm particularly predatory when it comes to my General Tso's chicken.

Channel surfing—a man's favorite pastime. If you want to know what goes on inside the brain of someone diagnosed with Attention Deficit Disorder, just sit on the sofa next to my husband and watch him flip through 400 channels in under one minute. There. Now you understand.

An over-stuffed refrigerator. I feel a sense of security and take personal pride in knowing that I've stockpiled enough food to survive WWIII, but let's face it—it's no fun digging through all of that food for the one jar of dill pickles at the very back of the fridge. No cravings and no amount of hunger are worth the avalanche that inevitably slides out of the refrigerator once I start rearranging the impossibly crammed shelves of yogurt, dog food, watermelon, and seven pounds of butter.

An empty toilet paper roll. Why do I never notice the roll is empty until *after* I've already completed my business on the toilet? I'm then forced to either drip dry or do the waddle of shame down the hallway to find a fresh roll.

Disappearing shampoo, soap, and towels. Nothing is worse than stepping into the shower and discovering that one, two, or all three of these items are missing from the stall. Even worse is having to run wet and naked through the house to find more, particularly when the doorbell rings and there are three Jehovah's Witnesses on the doorstep. Not my idea of fun.

Being home alone. Okay, this one actually isn't so bad—except when a spider the size of a giant calamari appears on my kitchen wall, and I'm forced to kill it by myself with an entire can of Raid.

Dishes that come out of the dishwasher dirtier than when they were put in. Every child who loads a dishwasher at night without first rinsing off the dishes is obviously working under the assumption that a kitchen fairy comes in the night and gleefully scrubs our crusty plates while we sleep.

An overflowing trash can. I've watched my kids purposefully stack trash next to the already full can in the hopes that the aforementioned kitchen fairy will wave her magic wand and *poof* the garbage away. By the time I give in and heft the plastic bag out of the can, it is so jam-packed that it inevitably splits, spilling the remnants of congealed leftovers onto the floor. Time to whistle for the dogs.

People who eat off my plate before I've finished my meal. Ever leave the room to answer the doorbell, and when you return to the table, your egg roll looks like it's been gnawed on by small rodents? I have. Many times.

Snoring. I can't sleep unless the only sound in the room is the soft whirring of a ceiling fan. This is unfortunate because lying next to my husband in bed is like sleeping in the middle of a rumbling thunderstorm, with a nearby pack of pigs rooting around for truffles. I've tried ear plugs. I've tried elbowing him in the ribs. I've tried pinching his nose closed until he wakes with a jolt from his cacophonous slumber, only for him to instantly growl and snuffle his way back to sleep. Of course, that's when the ceiling fan begins to wobble and clomp like the hooves of ten thousand stampeding horses. Hello, insomnia!

People who can't decide what fast food to order at the drive-through window. If I'm in a drive-through line at night, you better believe that my mouth is already watering for a burger or a chimichanga, and has been for some time. I cannot *stand* waiting behind a carload of rowdy partygoers arguing over which would taste better with booze—French fries or nachos. They'll be barfing up their takeout in a matter of hours, so what difference does it make? It all looks the same when it comes back up.

Bad cell phone reception. I can't tell you how many times my husband has called me from the hardware store to ask if I need anything, then instead of buying the box of light bulbs I asked for, he returns home with six hammers.

Slow drivers. These people are at their most irritating when I need to answer the call of nature—especially after I've eaten some questionable seafood. It never fails that I get stuck behind a Sunday driver on a Tuesday afternoon, two miles from the nearest restroom.

Stretch marks. I'm talking in particular about the angry red road maps left behind after giving birth. No matter how much Vitamin E you use, or how many lotions you try, or how much you pray to the God of Flat Perfect Tummies, they NEVER, EVER go away.

Vanishing cosmetics and fashion accessories. We're talking about things like hair spray, mascara, and under-eye concealer—items of no interest to my husband, sons, or dogs, which leaves only my daughters as potential culprits. I'm currently missing several sets of earrings, a dress, and two pairs of sandals. Thank God my girls aren't into culottes, neon Crocs, and plaid bathrobes—otherwise we'd have a war on our hands.

Still, as much as these things annoy me (and as much as I relish being annoyed by them) there are plenty of other things in this world that make me smile:

- Sipping a good Riesling while I kick back in the garden with my family and friends
- Sleeping in on Sunday mornings
- Eating fish and chips at Disney World's Rose & Crown Pub & Dining Room
- Slipping into cool, crisp sheets after a warm bath
- Watching the sun rise over the mountains in Wyoming
- Observing the interaction of squirrels and birds as they vie for seeds in the back yard
- Treating myself to movie-theater popcorn with extra butter (and a box of Snow Caps)
- Drinking a steaming cup of coffee from my favorite "I Love Squirrels" mug while sitting on my front porch and watching the world go by
- Feeling a renewed sense of hope and promise each and every Christmas morning
- Cuddling up with my husband on the couch late at night to watch old science fiction movies on TV.
- Spotting deer (and the occasional moose) outside my mother's kitchen window in Big Sky, Montana

- Drinking mimosas, seeing my husband lift a thirty-five pound turkey out of the oven, and watching *It's a Wonderful Life* on Thanksgiving morning.
- Sitting around the dining room table with all of my children, and listening to their side-splitting laughter as they recall some of our funniest family adventures
- Kissing my husband, which is the prelude to all things wonderful and mysterious in the bedroom
- Watching my husband dance to Beyoncé's "Single Ladies" while sporting his "Corn Poop—Life's Greatest Mystery" T-shirt, and feeling like the luckiest woman in the world.

The Joke's On Us

WE'VE ALL BEEN the victims of a prank at one time or another, and most likely we've pulled our own practical jokes on some other poor, unsuspecting souls. My family members and I are no exception. Over the years, we've made each other suffer through a wide variety of pranks—things like locking someone out of the house in his or her underwear, or shutting off the bathroom lights and leaving someone blind and soapy in the middle of an evening shower.

My youngest son wins the prize for being the biggest prankster in the family. Before he was even out of diapers, he'd already figured out how to dial 911, and one day he demonstrated these newfound telephone skills during one of my Tupperware parties. As twenty women "burped" rubber lids in my living room, the local police showed up at my front door, their badges flashing bright under the afternoon sun.

"A 911 call was received from your residence," they told me. "Do you mind if we take a look around the house to make sure you haven't injured yourself or the children?" Oh, I wanted to injure someone at that moment. You bet. (Side note: some of the ladies perked up considerably when the policemen entered the house. I think they believed they were going to be treated to an entirely different kind of party.)

By the time my little guy reached elementary school, he lived by the credo "Don't get mad, get even." One of his older sisters loved to whip him into a furious lather, constantly testing the limits of his sanity just to prove her sibling dominance over him. One such occasion occurred just after my son had left one of his overly large masterpieces in the toilet. I explained to him that, thrilled as I was that his pipes were in good working condition, it was not necessary to exhibit his work to the rest of the family. Then I pointed to the plunger and told him to have at it. Crinkling his nose in disgust, he flat-out refused to flush the largest bowel movement this side of the Mississippi.

We argued. I won. He plunged.

And his sister laughed.

He ignored her the first time, and when I noticed the dirty aftermath the plunger had left behind in the bowl, I handed my son the toilet brush to finish the job.

Again his sister laughed, and I sensed my son's inner lather being whipped.

Nevertheless, he scrubbed the toilet thoroughly until the bristles on the brush turned brown. Then, before I could remind him to rinse it off, he released a blood-curdling war cry that any nineteenth-century Native American would envy, flew at his sister with the brush, and baptized her in dirty, brown toilet water.

A good parent would have reprimanded her son for such a revolting retaliation against his sibling. A good parent would have made her son apologize to his sister profusely and beg her utmost forgiveness. A good parent would have demanded that he clean up his mess, preferably with a toothbrush, bucket, and pail. But I was *not* a good parent. I was too busy holding my sides together as they split apart in laughter.

My son's pranks didn't end there. Several years ago, when we owned a gift basket company in Fort Lauderdale, the holiday season was an especially stressful time for our family, and we had to hire additional help to pack baskets and run deliveries. We hired mostly teenagers to fill these positions, and sometimes they'd play pranks on one another at the work tables.

Observing this, my youngest son, who was six at the time, decided he wanted to get in on the games. He allowed the teenagers to tease him by sticking Christmas bows on his head and sealing him up in cardboard boxes with promises that they were shipping him to Antarctica. Little did they know that the kid had his own agenda—he would wait for just the right moment, squeeze hot glue onto a fake coin, and stick it on the arm of a teenage victim. That holiday season, many teenagers left our warehouse with hairless patches adorning their arms.

As my boy grew older, the pranks became more sophisticated. When his three older siblings would sleep late on the weekends, he'd tie their bedroom door handles together in the hallway, creating an intricate labyrinth out of string that would trap them inside their rooms. He would also rig cups full of water above the restroom door in order to soak any unfortunate person needing to answer the call of nature. And he took immense pleasure in leaving little surprises on his sisters' pillows: mummified lizards, dried-out cockroaches, and wads of used toilet paper.

But his all-time favorite prank at home was to tie a rubber band around the kitchen faucet. Aside from the regular hot and cold handles, our sink had an additional sprayer nozzle on the side. My son would rig it so that whoever turned the faucet on would be sprayed in the face from the third nozzle. The rubber band was carefully concealed and, by the end of any given day, everyone in the family fell victim to his watery trap.

(I knew it had gotten bad when my older sister expressed reservations about babysitting my son at her house—even when I assured her that he would be too distracted playing video games to get into any mischief.)

Although my youngest son is by far the biggest prankster in the family, he is not the only one who derives pleasure from "punking" others—my youngest daughter also enjoys humiliating people, especially when there's an audience on hand. One afternoon, when the two of us were standing in the checkout line, she polished off a jumbo-sized energy drink in record time and started acting squirrelly. I immediately recognized the feisty look in her eyes—it was one I'd seen many times before, and it meant: "I'm bored to death,

Mom. So I'm going to do something really stupid to entertain myself at your expense."

While my arms were filled with clothes and bags, my daughter realized she'd discovered the perfect opportunity to annoy the hell out of me while I was helpless to do anything about it. She started pinching my elbow, then worked her way up to the soft, flabby underside of my arm. I tried to discreetly push her away without causing a scene, but she continued to pinch and exasperate me. Eventually my cranky meter hit its limit, and I finally hissed at her to stop. She didn't hesitate, firing back loud enough for the entire lingerie department to hear, "MOM, YOU'RE SUCH A ROTTEN VAGINA!"

My face turned redder than a sun-dried tomato, and the middle-aged women in line behind me could scarcely contain their snickers. At that moment, it was easy to understand why some animals eat their young.

My husband has fallen prey to this same daughter's pranks on more than one occasion. A few years ago, during the holiday season, we stopped by Lowe's to check out the outdoor Christmas decorations. My daughter and I agreed that the lighted angel with the flapping wings was the prettiest and most appropriate item for our front yard. My husband smirked at our selection, informing us that the angel would soon be flapping her way into the trash can just as soon as the wires in her wings shorted out. It was his opinion that the lighted sleigh was far more practical.

And there it was again—the glint in my daughter's eye that told me the crowded aisle where we were standing was fueling her need to do something wicked. Knowing that something was coming, but not knowing exactly what it would be or when it would take place, I slowly edged my shopping cart down the aisle, as far away from the two of them as possible. I didn't want anyone to think I was actually related to the people arguing vehemently over the virtues of a flapping angel versus a rider-less sleigh.

"Dad, we all know the only reason you don't want the angel is because you're a SATAN WORSHIPPER!"

Thankfully, I managed to avoid the curious stares of the nearby shoppers by darting down Aisle Five to examine every size and shape of screwdriver Kobalt has ever produced.

My family has since learned that no one is immune to my girl's outrageous behavior in public. She exposes her quirky personality traits at the most inconvenient times, and thinks nothing of embarrassing not only her parents, but her siblings as well. She once joined her older sister's group of friends in the high school cafeteria and began complaining about the quality of the lunch food. Staring at the contents of her soggy tuna sandwich, she claimed it was unfit for consumption and flung it across the table. At her sister's face.

Without skipping a beat, my oldest daughter lifted the mayonnaise-soaked bread from her cheek and flung it back at her sibling. The other teenagers sat in stunned silence, their mouths forming perfect *o*'s. Later that week, when the other parents at the PTO meeting were bragging about their children's perfect test scores, I had to muster a smile and tell them how *my* wonderful daughters had almost started a Class A food fight in the school cafeteria.

My oldest daughter has her own particular way of exacting revenge on family members. At slumber parties, when she was younger, she would draw mustaches and sideburns on her sister's face in permanent marker. She once shaved off half of her little brother's eyebrows so dramatically that he resembled Dr. Spock on steroids. During her "I want to be a hairdresser" phase, she forced her younger sister to endure the humiliation of bangs cropped shorter than the newly-formed sprouts on a Chia Pet. She has even passed gas in crowded department stores, right before loudly proclaiming her disgust with me for letting one rip in a public place.

And let's not forget my oldest son, who tends to be more even-tempered than his siblings, and who is actually pretty sane when compared to the rest of us. He was the target of several interesting pranks during his college years, but it was hard to muster sympathy for him when I remembered that he was the one who convinced his seven-year-old brother to eat fifteen rum balls at our neighbor's Christmas party. There were many other things I would have rather been doing that night than cleaning chocolate vomit off of a tipsy second grader weaving around the living room like a college freshman at his first keg party. Yes, it was oddly comforting to know that my oldest son was getting pranked at college, and that he was receiving a great education in Karmic Retribution 101.

I'd never say that living in our house might be hazardous to someone's health, but I'd certainly warn them that it would be prudent to watch their backs while they're there. (And in case you're wondering how the Lowe's incident turned out, it was the angel with one single wing flapping who graced our front yard during Christmas that year.)

Vicious Cycle

OF MY GROUP OF FRIENDS, I was the last girl to get my period. To add insult to injury, I also spent more time in a training bra than most teenage girls in North America. I felt like I would never catch up to the other girls in my class. By the time I bought my first A-cup bra, they were already tossing aside their C-cups for D's.

While all of my friends were stocking up on sanitary napkins, I was still stocking up on Charms Pops, and wrappers for my gum chain. Every time one of the girls called to tell me she'd started her period, I would flush with envy. "Do you look different?" "Do you feel like a real woman now?" "Do you know you can get P-R-E-G-N-A-N-T?"

I was almost thirteen by the time I got my first period, and let me tell you, it was a big disappointment. Not that I was expecting a parade with balloons, confetti, and glittery tampons, but I expected *something*—even a nice dinner out with the family would have worked. I envisioned everyone around the table, their glasses held aloft, toasting my newfound menstrual cycle with a heartfelt "Welcome to womanhood!" But none of that happened.

I checked out my reflection ten times that day to see if I had changed. Nope. I was still a goofy-looking middle school student with braces and a little patch of sun freckles across my nose. It didn't help that my chest was as flat as a tortilla.

Honestly, though, none of that really mattered. All I cared about was the fact that I'd finally reached adolescence and earned the right to carry bulky cotton pads around in my purse. I could now sit in a circle during P.E. with all the other girls and complain about cramps, bloating, and menstrual mess. Best of all, I now had the perfect excuse to avoid doing things I disliked. I didn't have to run track. I didn't have to get into my bathing suit at swim parties where all the other girls were shaped like Barbie dolls. And if my mother happened to look in my drawer and discover the wrappers of fourteen World's Finest chocolate bars that I was supposed to sell in the band fundraiser, I could always blame the binge eating on my menses.

I also liked the power that my menstrual cycle granted me to manipulate certain situations. I could be moody or foul-mouthed and it didn't matter—everyone just blamed my bipolar behavior on my period. For one week out of each month, I had a license to act out, and then plead insanity caused by high hormonal levels. It was a dream come true.

The fun lasted for a while, until one day I got off the school bus and started walking home, and a group of boys behind me burst into laughter. I wondered what was so funny until I arrived home and discovered the dark stain spreading across my back side. That was the day I lost my power.

My period had betrayed me.

I was extremely paranoid and self-conscious after that, constantly checking my underwear at school for any unexpected visits from "Aunt Flo." I came to hate the fact that I had to schedule all of my activities around my period:

"I can't go to the beach today. If I get in the water I'll become a shark magnet!"

"I can't wear my new white sundress to the high school dance tonight. Someone might think I fell butt-first into the punch bowl!"

"Sorry, but this isn't really the best day for me to go to the mall and try on clothes."

A savvy group of girls in my middle school had learned to use tampons early on in their menstrual development. My circle of friends and I had some unsavory names for these girls, smug as we were in our certainty that there was only one possible reason they could shove tampons up their hoo-has with such ease. We secretly gossiped about them as we waddled down the school hallways in bulky pads the size of adult diapers. And we thought we were the smart ones!

Fortunately, as I grew older, my menses became more regular, and I stopped having to worry about nasty surprises in my underwear. I could pinpoint the day that my spotting would begin, and the calendar never lied. It made pregnancy planning pretty easy (except for my one "oops" baby, but that was the champagne's fault). If my period was even a day late, it meant one thing and one thing only—that I wasn't going to see it again for another nine months.

My cycle remained predictable until I hit middle age. Then, one day, my periods suddenly stopped. I missed a month and became terrified that I'd end up on the cover of *The National Enquirer* with the headline: "FIFTY-YEAR-OLD WOMAN GIVES BIRTH TO TRIPLETS—CLAIMS SHE NEVER KNEW SHE WAS PREGNANT!" I was on the verge of buying a home pregnancy kit when a close friend snapped me out of my momentary insanity by saying, "You're not pregnant, dummy, you're going through menopause!"

"Wait a minute," I cried. "You mean someone stole my period? Who stole my period? Was it that twelve-year-old down the block? She's wearing makeup and has breasts! I'll bet she stole it!"

I was just about ready to march down the street and claim rightful ownership over my period when the little voice of reason inside me said, "Marcia! Who cares? Let that little teeny bopper have your period. You're free. Free! Burn the tampons! Use the leftover maxi-pads as household sponges! Use the extra panty liners to remove your eye makeup! You're free!"

Sadly, my joy was short-lived, because it turned out that although my menstrual cycle had stopped, the symptoms had not. Every month at around the same time, I would undergo horrific mood swings, experience painful bloating and gas, and find myself tearing up over things like that maudlin ASPCA commercial featuring

Sarah McLachlan. The kids would run for cover at the first sign of my monthly hormone changes—I was Dr. Jekyll and Mrs. Hyde.

For months I lived period-free. I cleared the bathroom cabinets of all of my feminine products and started carrying smaller purses. All was well until the day I attended the local Renaissance festival. It was an unusually warm day, and I was dressed in all of my Renaissance finery—hoop skirt, slips, lace, the works. I felt the urge to pee, so I crammed myself into a tight, dirty Porta-Potty, and guess who came knocking at the door? Yup. It was Good ol' Aunt Flo, back from an extended vacation in Bermuda, and there was nary a tampon in sight.

It was a horrible period that lasted ten days (or was it ten months?) and drained me of all energy and enthusiasm for life. Even chocolate did nothing to lift my spirits. When my period did finally fade away, I held onto my last box of tampons like a shield, just in case Mother Nature had any more surprises up her sleeve.

Another six months passed, and it was time for my daughter's college graduation. I was so excited to get out of town for a few days and see my daughter receive her diploma. The suitcases were stuffed into the car, and after a final check of the locks and lights, I took one last trip to the bathroom before hitting the road. Sure enough, the evil demon had returned! But this time I was prepared. I blew the dust off my box of tampons and tossed them into the car. The Red Sea was not going to keep me from visiting my daughter.

The way I see it, I'm due for another period sometime during the holiday season. Maybe even on Christmas Day—or perhaps Aunt Flo will be too busy skiing in Colorado to bother me.

The calendar never lies.

Or does it?

Menopause:
The Good, the Bad, and the Ugly

IF YOU TURN ON your computer and google "symptoms of menopause," you'll probably find a list of the traits that define a woman on the brink of menopausal insanity, and a picture of my face directly underneath it. Menopause set up camp in my uterus several years ago and hasn't vacated the premises since. After all, why should it leave when it can just pull up a chair, make itself comfortable, and wave goodbye to my estrogen levels while they pack their bags and flee for younger ground? That's when the real fun begins, and Mother Nature wants a front-row seat.

If you're a middle-aged woman experiencing any of the following symptoms, I'd say that menopause is getting ready to set up house in your lady parts and turn your Fertile Crescent into the Mojave Desert:

Hot Flashes. Summer has gone from "fun in the sun" to "hiding in your house with the air conditioning on full blast." Winter is your new favorite time of year—you may be trapped in Hell's sauna with no way out, but at least your hot flashes help keep the heating bill low. (They also help you sweat out the extra calories from the chocolate Nutty Buddy cones you scarf down in your car every time you go to the gas station.)

Weight Gain. You've had to break into your savings account for a brand new wardrobe that includes an abundance of spandex undergarments, pants with elastic waistbands, and those knee-length muumuus that are wildly popular at outlet stores. Enjoying a well-deserved beach vacation? Be careful when you squeeze into your new tankini—strangers are going to want to rub your Buddha belly for good luck.

There are definitely plus sides to those few additional pounds, however, especially if the extra weight is distributed in the right places. If it goes to your breasts, you've got a built-in flotation device—no more worries about drowning in the ocean! If it settles in your badonkadonk, you can sign up as a backup dancer for Beyoncé's next music video. Sadly, though, if the excess weight takes up residence in your stomach, you'll have to tell everyone that you have an inoperable tumor in your belly.

Mood Swings. You're envious of your bipolar aunt—at least she's on meds to balance out her emotions, and she always has a smile on her face. You, on the other hand, feel like Mother Teresa one minute and Attila the Hun the next.

Night Sweats. You've learned to appreciate swimming at night because you're frequently hot and uncomfortable in the warm, sticky puddle that was once your bed. The tradeoff to waking up on sheets drenched in sweat is that you no longer wake up on sheets drenched in menstrual blood. No more period means you can swim with Great Whites and not become fish bait, camp in the mountains without fear of grizzly bears shredding your tent, and walk down the beach without a flock of seagulls trailing behind you. Worth it.

Low Libido. Your vagina has become a sand trap, and your sex drive is like that of a spayed animal. The good news? At least you no longer have to feign headaches when you're not in the mood for a tussle under the covers. Just remind your spouse that your lady parts are as dry as tumbleweeds rolling across Death Valley, and he'll be certain to leave you alone.

Hair Loss. Your hair is losing its grip on your head so rapidly that you could probably open a wig shop with the fallout. Pretty soon you'll be checking out Pinterest for crafty ideas on how to weave lost bits of hair into useful household items such as placemats and napkin rings.

Memory Loss. Your house is wallpapered in Post-it notes reminding you to brush your teeth, turn off the stove, and flush the toilet. You check the locks five times after stepping out the front door, and jiggle the handle of your car incessantly to make sure the locks are engaged. You arrive at the grocery store only to realize you have no idea what prompted you to go there in the first place.

Relax. Memory loss is a normal side effect of menopause, so why not try to look at it from a positive angle? Your brain will finally begin whittling away at all of those nasty movie reels from the past—you know, the ones you'd rather forget? Like the night you puked spiked orange juice all over your best friend's bed at a sorority party. Or the time your husband thought it was a good idea to clear the dance floor at your cousin's wedding reception by doing "The Worm" in his tuxedo.

Fatigue. Your body shifts into narcoleptic mode every day after lunch when you discover that the coffee pot in the office break room is empty. To combat the fatigue, you're going to have to start making regular runs to Starbucks—or you could try to convince your boss that you have a medical condition which requires a midday nap. Either way, be sure to carry a pillow with you at all times.

Anxiety. Everything makes you feel anxious. You grind your teeth in your sleep like an agitated badger, and your manicure looks like you've been trailing your fingertips across the surface of a piranha pool. The good news is that you no longer need to worry about getting pregnant at this stage of life. All the money you would have normally spent on birth control can now be put towards a year's supply of Viagra.

Indigestion. Every time you eat dinner at your favorite Mexican restaurant, you end up feeling as if someone lit a handful of Roman candles and dropped them down your throat. When you get home, resist the urge to yell "FIRE IN THE HOLE!" before beating a path to the bathroom. At least that fiery food is guaranteed to clean out your insides better than colon hydrotherapy.

Frequent Urination. Your car trips are mapped out according to how many pit stops there are between your driveway and your destination. Everyone knows that the humongous purse you carry around is really the equivalent of an adult diaper bag, offering a fashionable place to tuck your endless supply of pee pads.

Dry Skin. Menopause dries out the skin, and as a result, dark patches can sometimes tarnish your otherwise immaculate complexion. Great news! This is your excuse to spend a fortune at the Lancôme counter. No one wants to look in the mirror and see a face that resembles a ten-year-old Shar Pei.

Menopause is a fact of womanhood, and how you handle it is all in the attitude. It's known as "the change of life," not the END of life, and the reality is that it's not all bad. You just have to learn how to roll with the night sweats, bloating, and messy mood swings. (It doesn't hurt to have a healthy stock of wine on hand at all times. And a box fan, just in case.)

Congratulations! It's a Food Baby!

WHEN MY DAUGHTER was nineteen weeks pregnant with her first baby, she asked me to accompany her to the obstetrician's office for her checkup. Thank God I brought enough food and water to last a week on a deserted island, because the waiting room was PACKED. I was surrounded by young women in various stages of pregnancy, and as I sat there sweating through a hot flash and fanning myself with a wrinkled baby magazine, I realized I was the only fossil in the room. I even saw the women at the reception desk giving me a funny looks. "What's the old lady doing here? Giving birth to a dinosaur egg?"

I self-consciously rubbed my stomach and remembered the good old days when there was actually a living creature in there. Now the only thing I'm growing is a food baby. You know what I'm talking about—men have them, too, though theirs are called beer bellies. For women, they're food babies, and they're the accumulations of every nacho, corn dog, and glass of chardonnay we consume between the clandestine bites of chocolate we carefully hide from our children.

It's God's little joke on women—all because Eve took one bite out of that damn apple. Unless they have the metabolism of Speedy Gonzales or a body like a Disney Princess, most middle-aged females I know get what my mother fondly refers to as "the pouch" after their babies are born.

I myself have been carrying around my food baby for years, and so have most women my age. Imagine a group of us sitting on a park bench discussing our "pregnancies." Here's how the conversation might unfold:

"So how far along are you?"

"Oh, we started back in 1986."

"How nice! When are you due?"

"Well, I'm not too sure. Maybe when I start the South Beach Diet."

"I don't think mine wants to be born at all."

"What kind of baby are you having?"

"Mine is a sausage and pepperoni pizza baby."

"Mine is taco dip and cheese enchiladas."

"We're going to be the proud parents of cheese fries."

"Mine is Ben & Jerry's ice cream. I think I'm having twins!"

Thinking about food babies while sitting in the obstetrician's waiting room reminded me that I needed to feed mine, so I nibbled on a breakfast bar and read an article about diaper rashes, diarrhea, and colic. I smiled. My daughter had no idea what she'd gotten herself into.

One hour and three breakfast bars later, I had a front row seat to a gynecological show that involved my daughter lifting herself up onto the examining table and putting her feet up into the stirrups. I looked at everything else in the room except THAT.

Hearing my future grandchild's heartbeat for the first time brought back a flood of memories. My last pregnancy was nineteen years ago (though it feels more like sixty) and time has thankfully dulled my memories of labor pains and C-sections. Yet I distinctly recall the sweet and simple things: my favorite blue, polka-dotted maternity outfit, the circus clown lantern in the nursery, and how incredibly good a Reuben sandwich tasted after experiencing intense pregnancy cravings. Sleepless nights, fold-up umbrella strollers, bulky car seats, lost bottles, tears, pacifiers, the smell of baby powder, panicky calls to the pediatrician at all hours—these other things are all a blur.

My daughter was once a tiny baby swaddled in pink, and now, here she was, all grown up and pregnant with a child of her own. I thought of how my own body had changed over the past few years, and how menopause had slowly crept in and stolen my fertility. Some women view menopause as a youth-stealing thief, while others experience a greater sense of freedom. Regardless of one's personal philosophy, it's my opinion that menopause should not define who we are. It's simply a time of change and enlightenment.

Even though I felt older than dirt that morning among all of the young, fresh-faced mothers in the obstetrician's office, I appreciated the chance to take stock of my past and evaluate who I am today. Yes, I'm more tired, more impatient, more emotional, and my body aches most mornings before my feet even hit the floor. I'm a sometimes-grumpy woman who has hot flashes in elevators, denies herself that last slice of chocolate cake she so desperately craves, and wastes precious time searching the house for things her kids have "borrowed" but never returned. Despite all of this, I still wear many happy hats: cook, dishwasher, maid, chauffeur, tutor, therapist, budget planner, dog walker, party planner, hostess, and family organizer. Above all else, I'm a mother and a grandmother.

And after last night, the proud parent of a beef and bean burrito food baby.

Blessings

WHEN SOMEONE ASKS me what the best times in my life have been, I'm always at a loss for what to say, because I've experienced so many spectacular moments that it is impossible for me to choose just a few that stand out above the rest.

Likewise, there have been many heart-wrenching moments that have also shaped me in ways I never imagined possible: holding my baby boy in my arms just moments before he died; laying my head against my father's chest and hearing his heartbeat slow until it stopped; joking on the phone one day with my sister, not realizing it was the last time I'd hear her voice.

Yet of all the joy that has lifted us up over the years, and of all the heartbreak that has saddened us while turning us into stronger people, my husband and I agree that some of the most magical moments we've shared together were the ones spent in the labor and delivery room.

Labor was long and intense with my first baby. I spent most of the night enduring wave after wave of painful contractions. Finally, after a late-night bathroom break, I eased myself off of the toilet only to have Niagara Falls gush forth onto the carpet. I yelled for my husband in a panic: "I CAN'T STOP PEEING!"

After that point, there is a serious divergence in what I remember about the blessed event and what my husband remembers. I have vivid memories of grabbing tight fistfuls of my husband's shirt while bravely huffing, puffing, and swearing like a sailor. My husband recalls a much more dramatic scene—a reenactment of *The Exorcist*, starring his wife in the role of Regan, complete with spinning head, pasty face, and demonic voice.

Fifteen hours later, my oldest son was born, but I didn't get a chance to see his eyes until later that evening, when he opened them for the first time. Startling and vivid blue, his eyes sparkled like sapphires, and in their azure depths I saw a glimpse of the man my newborn son would eventually become—intelligent, handsome, and kind.

I brought him home from the hospital and was hit with the realization that I had no idea how to raise a child. But after locking myself in the bathroom for a good cry, it occurred to me that my infant son was new to this whole mother/baby relationship too. We would learn and grow together, holding onto one another as we navigated the uncharted territory of new parenthood.

My second child was born after an extremely difficult pregnancy, and as such, her arrival was a moment of both elation and intense relief. The nurse laid my baby daughter against my chest, and it was at that moment that I noticed the double dimples creasing her left cheek. I laughed through my tears and pulled her closer to my heart, experiencing both profound gratitude and joy while at the same time grieving desperately for her lost twin brother. My second baby was my miracle baby, and she became my rock through the dark hours of sorrow and anguish that followed.

Today my fiercely independent daughter walks down the path of new parenthood hand in hand with her own baby girl, and her grasp seems so much stronger and more confident than my own at that age. I couldn't be prouder of the woman she has become.

My husband and I still chuckle at our memories of the birth of our third child. That was the pregnancy in which I took the conventional "eating for two" wisdom to new heights, and my daughter, despite arriving two weeks ahead of schedule, weighed a whopping nine-and-a-half pounds. Thank God she didn't go full-term, or else I would have given birth to the newborn equivalent of a fourteen-pound

Butterball turkey. She was the largest baby in the nursery; when the nurses swaddled her, she looked like a tiny sumo wrestler.

My little would-be-Butterball has now turned into a graceful swan with a great sense of humor, an infectious laugh, and a smile that can light up a room. She always provides the dose of sunshine I need to keep my own positive attitude going when life isn't always so kind.

Our last baby decided to make an early appearance into the world, which put a serious crimp in my plans that day; I was forced to deliver Thanksgiving cookies to my older son's elementary school class with amniotic fluid trickling down my legs. To this day, my youngest boy is still as impulsive and impatient as he was at the very beginning, ready to grab onto life with both hands and enjoy the ride. He stresses me to the point of craving tequila by noon each day, but his compassion, brilliance, and love of life never cease to amaze and inspire me.

Overall, I am thankful for each and every one of my children, and I could not feel more blessed to be a part of this crazy, funny family that has gifted me with such unforgettable moments over the years. It would be impossible for me to pick just one, two, or even a handful of these moments as being the best times in my life. Our lives together form an ongoing tapestry of laughter and love, and the memories we share will resonate for years to come through the lives of our grandchildren.

The Bright Side of a Storm

EVERY YEAR, WHEN the hurricane season comes to an end, you can hear a collective sigh of relief in the sun-splashed streets of our neighborhood. We are no longer glued to The Weather Channel to see if the "cone of concern" has moved an inch further in our direction. We don't need to stockpile bottles of water, flashlight batteries, and cans upon cans of Chef Boyardee. The plywood comes down from the windows, and we emerge like groundhogs from the dark holes of our homes to embrace the bright, blessed fall mornings of South Florida.

Every day, when I stand at the edge of my backyard to survey its beautiful landscaping, I'm reminded of the destruction wrought on our community in 2004 by Hurricane Frances. My carefully planned garden was destroyed when our sixty-five-foot ficus tree was pulled from the earth, uprooting half of the landscaping and popping up the pathway bricks like popcorn kernels. My meticulous garden looked like a good candidate for an HGTV yard improvement show.

The morning after Hurricane Frances, it was too early for me to stress over the mutilated garden, or the power outage that had shrouded my boarded-up home in darkness. My brain was muddled and I needed caffeine. Sadly, the only restaurant in the area still humming with electricity had a long line of thirty people, all of whom were also in the throes of caffeine withdrawal. I never realized how much I depended on coffee until the threat of not having it consumed me.

My husband and I were driving around aimlessly in search of a coffee fix when I suddenly remembered our generator. It was a brand-new, candy-apple-red model, just waiting for that first test drive. Had my husband and I read the directions? Of course not, but that didn't matter. All I cared about was the extension cord that would hook that sucker up to my coffee machine, so that I could contemplate with a clear head all of the life changes that were about to take place in the absence of electricity.

After coffee, our next priority was the air conditioning. With the help of our generator, we were able to hook up a small cooling unit in the living room, where our entire family of six was camped out on the floor. It was fun at first, but the novelty of "roughing it" wore off after about an hour, once it dawned on the kids that there would be no TV, no cell phone service, and no video games. They were also heartbroken to learn that McDonald's doesn't use fleets of generators to keep the deep fryers running during weather emergencies.

By early afternoon, there were bright orange extension cords snaking across the streets where neighbors (some of whom hadn't seen or spoken to each other in months) had magnanimously decided to share their generators with one another. Such displays of generosity stirred something in my heart, restoring my faith in the kindness of others. Sharing coolers filled with beer and rum also helped boost neighborhood morale.

Despite the inconveniences, the storm also had its benefits. Instead of staring at a blaring television in the evenings, our family would gather around the kerosene lantern to play Uno and Monopoly. And for the first time in years, I didn't worry once about my diet. What better excuse than a hurricane to break out the junk food? Without an ounce of guilt, I raided the hurricane emergency box for my daily dose of Pringles and peppermint patties. It was too dark in the house to read the numbers on the bathroom scale anyway, so a side dish of Cheetos with some thawed-out hamburger patties seemed perfectly acceptable. I wasn't alone in my thinking—most people I spoke with after the storm said they'd gained five pounds during the week we lived without power. There was no sense letting all the food in the freezer go to waste, so why not eat mass quantities of it for the brief time it could still be heated on the grill?

Along with weight-loss concerns, our beauty concerns also flew out the window. Blow dry our hair? Not unless we wanted to blow up our generator. We learned to stick our heads out the car window while speeding down the highway in order to achieve that special wind-blown look. Without electricity, there was also no water heater, which meant our days of hot showers were suspended. We adapted to the life of our early ancestors, and enjoyed what we fondly referred to as "Karate Chop Showers"—the quick slicing of limbs through icy water, topped off with fast, eye-opening head dunks.

During that week without power, we came to think of our generator no longer as a machine, but as the lifeline to our creature comforts. At times, our dependency on it was frightening. We arranged our schedules so that someone was always at home to keep the generator running. Every three hours it needed a gas refill. In the middle of the night when it would shut off, there was always an argument over whose turn it was to "feed the baby."

Living without power is not the only thing I associate with the aftermath of Hurricane Frances, however. Certain sounds from that period in my life will remain forever ingrained in my memory. The heavy rumble of the Florida Power and Light trucks became synonymous with hope for the restoration of electricity. One day, after sweating in a ninety-degree house, I lost all dignity and chased after a power truck. Looking back, I think that being cooped up in a hot, dark room with a bunch of sweaty people who hadn't showered for days was more than enough reason for such an act of desperation. At that point, I was prepared to sell my youngest child for a day's worth of air conditioning.

Another peculiar sound I'll never forget was that of the grinding claws of the bulk trash trucks as they drove around collecting and compacting roadside debris. The scraping of metal against pavement and wood made a noise that sounded more like Arctic beasts chewing on bones than something as ordinary as giant trash mashers.

In contrast to the garbage compactors, however, I found comfort in the humming sound of our neighbors' generators as they chugged steadily throughout the night. It was the only noise to break the eerie silence in our dark and desolate neighborhood, where no street lights shone. For the first time in as long as we could remember, we were able to see the pinpoints of light from thousands of stars above, and the constellations were easily identifiable without a telescope.

A week later, when the electricity was finally restored, I found myself a little disappointed that life would soon return to normal. Though I will admit, when I stepped into that first warm shower in my brightly-lit bathroom, I could have sworn I heard the angels singing.

The time came for us to face the daunting task of restoring our yard, which meant the removal of the large ficus tree. We had a tree-trimming party with the neighbors—all of whom came bearing electric saws and pizza. Watching my favorite tree being reduced to fireplace logs was disconcerting, and in a strange way, it felt as if I'd lost an old friend. Despite the overall bonhomie of the tree-trimming party, I felt sad every time I looked at the deep crater in the center of my yard.

A month later, however, friends and family surprised us with three live oak trees and armloads of flowering plants, all of which quickly restored the peace and tranquility of my backyard garden. As with the sharing of the generators, it was humbling to witness the kindness of people drawn together by an instinctive need to help.

Hurricanes are a fact of life in Florida, and each year from June until November we brace ourselves for "The Big One," praying it will never land on our coastline. But if it does, I'll be ready with a pantry full of canned ravioli, bottled water, and a new generator large enough to power the entire block.

Maybe then I'll get the chance to use up all of those bags of Cheetos stashed in the back of my closet.

How to Annoy Your Children

FROM THE MOMENT they're born, our children are tremendous sources of personal pride for us. From their first words and first steps, to the gold stars on their progress reports, to their starring roles in school plays and musicals—we are always there for them, cheering them on, sharing their accomplishments with anyone willing to listen.

Our children are reflections of ourselves, and often their behavior is what people use to assess our parenting skills. When they're giggling toddlers passing gas on a crowded elevator, everyone thinks they're adorable. As sixteen-year-olds competing in belching contests at a five-star restaurant? Not so much.

Let's face it—the older our children get, the more embarrassing they become. They transform from cute, cuddly puppy dogs into snapping, snarling beasts that act like they've been raised in the woods by wild boars. They curse like sailors and their vocabulary becomes a series of primitive grunts, groans, and the occasional "whatever" shrugs. They eat mass quantities of food that cause the grocery bill to soar; sweets and chips are the largest part of their food pyramid, though milk and juice are also consumed at an alarming rate, usually at about a gallon per child per day.

As a parent your children once adored and respected, you now represent a large source of embarrassment to them. It is with great pleasure (and an utter lack of conscience) that they choose to retaliate by publicly annoying and humiliating you. They gleefully belch and fart in crowded rooms and point fingers at any unsuspecting parent nearby. They tell their grandparents that there are only three ingredients in their refrigerator at home: one grayish-looking egg, a carton of sour milk, and a moldy brick of cheddar cheese that looks like last year's school science fair project. Naturally, the grandparents take pity on the children's pour souls and drive them to the nearest McDonald's.

- Every parent reaches a breaking point with their children eventually. A time comes when they need to liberate themselves from the bonds of "politically correct" child-rearing and just *get even*. The following is a payback list that has been especially effective for us in annoying our teenagers, and will most likely be successful in annoying yours:
- Crank up the lawn mower outside their bedroom window when they're trying to sleep late on a Saturday morning.
- Ask twenty questions about the TV show they're watching, but wait until they're immersed in the thickest part of the plot.
- During one of your teenager's house parties, run into the room with a dripping wet plunger in your hand and shout: "Okay, who clogged the toilet?"
- Pick up the six wet towels the child has left on the bathroom floor and deposit them into his or her unmade bed, being sure to tuck the towels under the covers first so everything stays nice and moist.
- Allow your youngest child to bang on his new drum set while his older siblings are trying to nap.
- Turn on the sprinklers while your daughter is sunbathing in the back yard.
- At neighborhood block parties, jump up on a table after a couple of beers and play air guitar to Bon Jovi songs.
- Call your son's friends "Dude" and "Bro."
- Write embarrassing messages on their Facebook walls: "Did you eat that WHOLE package of Oreos I hid in the pantry?" "Why is all my underwear missing from the dryer?"

- Blast Barry Manilow on the car radio while driving your kids and their friends to school, making sure that all the windows are rolled down so EVERYONE in the car loop can hear you belting out the lyrics to "Mandy."
- At your son's sixteenth birthday party, borrow his best friend's BMX bike and show those young whippersnappers how to fly over a speed bump and rack yourself on the bicycle seat.
- Write a book about your family life, and highlight all the personal stuff that will make your kids cringe and want to disown you.

Revenge has never been sweeter!

Just Say "No" to Horror Movies

I'VE NEVER UNDERSTOOD why people love horror movies. I don't enjoy getting the crap scared out of me, or pooping my pants in fright. My kids thrive on "jump scare" movies, but if *my* heart needs a jump start, it's going to come from a medical professional slapping some paddles on my chest and yelling: "CLEAR!"

The Exorcist hit the box office when I was in middle school. All the cool kids crammed into the theaters on opening weekend, but my mother refused to let me see the movie—though that probably had more to do with Linda Blair stuffing a crucifix up her nether regions than the actual demonic possession.

Fast forward ten years to the release of *Poltergeist*. I didn't WANT to see this movie, but it was the talk of the town and I'd be damned if I was going to miss out on all the fun. BIG MISTAKE. My bladder muscles have never been the same, and no amount of Kegel exercises are going to get my pelvic floor back into shape. *Poltergeist* convinced me that my home was built over an ancient Native American burial ground, and that I'd be sucked into my television set by demonic spirits. Because of that movie, I haven't slept without a night light since 1982.

For years after *Poltergeist*, I lived in blissful ignorance of popular horror movies, until my teenagers convinced me to watch *The Ring*. "Yeah, let's scare the shit out of Mom and shave a few years off her life!" If they wanted early access to their inheritance, they could have done it in a more humane way than telling me that movie was "not at all scary."

Being the naïve parent I was, I fell for their sadistic plot to give me early gray hairs, and watched *The Ring*. Suffice it to say, I spent the following two hours chewing on my cuticles until my fingers looked like they'd been through a cheese grater. I spent WEEKS afterwards sitting up late at night, just waiting for a creepy girl with stringy black hair to come crawling out of my television set. That movie was my introduction to Mr. Insomnia, and we've been carrying on a cozy affair ever since.

Don't get me wrong, I'm not a total wuss. I can watch *The Walking Dead* and *American Horror Story*—as long as every light in the house is on and all the doors are locked. And it doesn't hurt to barter sex with my husband for extra assurances that there are no zombies roaming my backyard in search of brains, and no creepy dudes in black latex suits hiding in my closet.

Paranormal Activity, *Saw*, and *Carrie*? No, no, and HELL no. Unless the theater provides free JELL-O shots and a Depends undergarments dispenser, don't expect to see me in line for the next Halloween horror hit.

You Are What You Eat

I'VE BEEN ON SOME kind of diet since the day I graduated from Gerber pureed peaches to actual grown-up food. By the time I was five, I'd already discovered the joys of a chocolate-induced endorphin high. When we were young, my sister and I would routinely sneak out of the house on Saturday mornings, hide behind a thick hedge in Kester Park, and eat Reese's Peanut Butter Cups.

My sister was a master at hiding candy from my parents. She taught me the art of stuffing my fancy church socks with penny candies and hiding packets of M&M's in my doll house. At the age of six, candy consumption had already given me a beer belly, many years before I even knew what beer was. Little did I know that this was the beginning of a lifelong battle of the bulge.

The Golden Arches didn't open their doors in our town until I was in middle school, but once they did, I yearned for those Big Macs with special sauce, and I ached to make up for lost time. Fortunately for me, the styles that were fashionable during my McDonald's years included baggy elephant pants and blousy peasant shirts, which carefully masked the extra chub I accumulated from my frequent visits to Ronald McDonald's place.

By the time I reached high school, however, my desire to have a boyfriend far outweighed my love for anything deep-fried or sautéed in butter. I bought a tiny food scale and began weighing every crumb that passed my lips, all so I could squeeze into a bodysuit and a pair of stove pipe jeans—clothing that left nothing to the imagination.

Over the years, the bathroom scale has alternated between being my worst critic and the object of an unhealthy obsession. "Diet" has become a nasty four-letter word that conjures in my mind images of banana slices, dry whole-wheat toast, and boiled chicken breasts so small they could easily double as shoulder pads or brassiere inserts. When I think diet, I think low-carb, low-fat, low-calorie, and no flavor—in other words, living on lettuce leaves and feeling more and more like a rabbit each day. I try to eat low-cal foods slowly so they'll magically shrink my appetite, but this is difficult to do while watching my sons devour slice after slice of pepperoni pizza. There are days when I would sell my left kidney for a large Domino's supreme.

You name the diet, I've tried it: South Beach, Atkins, Slim-Fast, Sugar Busters, and The Zone. I've also done the soup diet, the grapefruit diet, and the liquid Hollywood diet that makes absurd promises about helping you lose five pounds in one day. (This last one is great if you plan to attend your high school reunion in a slinky, size six dress. But be sure to wear a girdle, because the minute you pop a canapé into your mouth, your stomach will rise faster than the Pillsbury Doughboy in a four-hundred-degree oven.)

I've also gone the route of laxatives and water pills (not healthy, very dangerous, and certainly not a good idea unless you enjoy spending 85 percent of your day on the toilet), and I've suffered many grueling hours at the gym. If I sat and calculated all the miles I've run on a treadmill since I was twenty-five, I bet I've been around the world at least ten times—without the benefit of tasting the exotic cuisines from each country.

The doctors say that with dieting, it's all about portion control, and that each meal we eat should be no larger than a fist. If that's true, I wish I were the size of the Jolly Green Giant. Have you seen *his* fist?

One of my favorite diets was Atkins. What other diet allows you to eat pork rinds and salads coated with bleu cheese dressing? It was great—until I cheated with one slice of birthday cake as thin as a feather. The next day my evil scale reflected a five-pound weight gain. How was it possible to gain weight that quickly? Could one slice of cake really weigh five pounds? I ended my relationship with Atkins that day, and consoled myself with the remainder of the cake.

Not only have I watched the numbers yo-yo on my scale, but I've watched them fluctuate in my closet as well. Ask any female—we all own at least two different wardrobes (and I don't mean summer and winter). We have our fat clothes and our skinny clothes, and the wardrobe *de jour* is dictated by the numbers on the scale each morning. Binged on Ferrero Rocher chocolates and Fettuccine Alfredo yesterday? Today's outfit will be loose-fitting pants and a blousy top. Eat nothing but yogurt and carrot sticks today? You can be sliding into tight jeans and that little knit sweater tomorrow. (This strategy works fine as long as you don't go overboard on the Fettuccine Alfredo days—otherwise you'll be bringing in Omar the Tent Maker to design you a new wardrobe.)

For years my morning mantra has been "Nothing tastes as good as skinny feels," but this notion is often sorely challenged, particularly when I'm invited to a party and, instead of checking out the hot guys, I end up checking out the buffet table. Who cares about the Johnny Depp look-alike in the corner when there are pigs in a blanket and loaded nachos calling my name?

When my husband and I were first married, Sunday dinner was always held at my parents' home, where the whole family would gather around the pot roast. It didn't take long for my husband to reach the conclusion that my family was obsessed with food. It confused and disturbed him that the bulk of our table conversation revolved around the meals we'd eaten during the week, the restaurants we'd visited, and the new recipes we'd tried.

"How can you talk about Lobster Thermidor," he'd ask, "while you're still in the middle of eating pork chops with plum sauce?" My sisters and I would just share a knowing glance. It wasn't long before my husband was calling me from work at 11:00 a.m. each day to ask what I was planning for dinner. He liked knowing what would be on the table when he got home, so that he'd have something to look forward to during the long hours at the office.

As newlyweds, my husband had to suffer through a lot of my early experiments in the kitchen—some of which were, quite frankly, disastrous (think cream sauces that could be used as wallpaper paste and vegetables mushy enough to consume without dentures.) However, now that I'm an accomplished cook and have earned myself the title of "Casserole Queen," my man isn't satisfied unless the food on his plate is piled higher than Mount Everest.

Marrying into a food-obsessed household has unfortunately had its disadvantages for my husband. He is finally facing something that most of us have already accepted by the time we hit forty— unwanted belly fat. Our stomachs are now the dumping ground for every beer, cheese puff, and bowl of ice cream we've consumed since our bar-hopping days. (I'll admit I'm still a sucker for those TV commercials that advertise pills made to reduce stubborn belly fat, especially during the dreaded swimsuit season. Sadly, such pills aren't designed to work in conjunction with a diet of grilled cheese sandwiches and chips.)

Despite my family history, my children seem to have a much better handle on their eating habits than I ever did. They don't feel the urge to hide their candy in socks or pillowcases, they haven't inherited my lumberjack appetite, and they don't seem to have any interest in yo-yo dieting. But they DO have my sweet tooth, and a keen curiosity about the contents of my grocery bags after I come home from the weekly shopping trip.

If anything, my children have become pickier eaters during their teenage and adult years. It doesn't matter if I've spent fifty dollars or three hundred and fifty dollars at the grocery store—either way, they'll whine and say there's nothing good to eat in the house. If I suggest they try cooking something, they look at me as if I've just offered them scrapple, and then race out the door for the nearest sushi bar.

(My youngest son has a different approach to food. He likes to open the refrigerator every five minutes in the hopes that something wonderful and new has appeared on its frosty shelves since the last time he looked. One time he stood there so long that I thought my husband had installed cable TV on the cold racks.)

You can't chew on something while walking through our house without someone asking, "What are you eating?" Which is usually followed by, "Can I have a bite?" All I have to do is walk into the kitchen, crinkle some paper, and inevitably one of the kids will yell from the next room, "I want some!" Little do they know I'm opening up a bag of pellets for my pet chinchillas.

Lately, I've come to terms with my food addiction, and I'm happy just to maintain my weight. I've accepted the fact that I'll never be as skinny as I was during the Fen-Phen craze. Although my kitchen shelves are lined with dozens of cookbooks, I'm content to munch on lettuce leaves and celery, just as long as I know there's a pint of Häagen-Dazs in my future.

Over the Hill and Away We Go

I DON'T LIKE MORNINGS. I wake up feeling like Rip Van Winkle— thirty years gone in the blink of an eye—and I'm out of energy, out of touch, and out of style. The whole experience of getting out of bed makes me feel older than dirt.

The other day I complained to my mother that my right hip was starting to ache after my morning walk. "Bursitis!" my mother said, with a knowing grin. When I complained about the stiffness that occurs in my fingers late at night, she said, "Arthritis!" and recommended some medications. Bursitis? Arthritis? Really? That kind of stuff only happens to OLD people, and I'm not old—yet.

If any of the following items apply to you, it's time to admit that you might be over the hill:

The calendar that was once filled with social engagements is now filled with doctor appointments.

You're addicted to HGTV and the Food Network.

Sunburns are out; hot flashes are in.

You need to apply deodorant more than once a day.

You've had to discard your thongs and other sexy lingerie in favor of foundation garments—the more spandex, the better.

Naps are the highlight of your day.

You once stood in line for tickets to Guns N' Roses; now you stand in line for a flu shot.

You're still using a VCR to record your favorite shows.

The music playing in elevators and at the dentist's office is the same stuff you danced to in the 1970s and 1980s.

Hangovers last longer than one day.

You still use a phone book to look up phone numbers.

You know what triglycerides are, and you monitor them carefully.

Everything in your wardrobe is made with elastic.

You need caffeine to keep you awake during the day, and Lunesta to fall asleep at night.

You look in the mirror and realize you are JUST LIKE YOUR PARENTS!

In a Flash

WHEN I WAS IN middle school, I would hear my mother and her friends discussing their hot flashes, and assume they were referring to something scandalous. The term "hot flash" suggested many things to my younger self; in my hormonal, thirteen-year-old mind, I was convinced that it was a blaze of lust. Is it any wonder that I cringed whenever I heard older women discussing their hot flashes in intimate detail?

By the time I was in my early twenties, I had a better understanding of what hot flashes were, but I gave them little thought, believing them to be a problem that only concerned women older than dinosaurs. I surmised these women to be the very same ladies who clustered under ceiling fans at parties, and swiped all the dinner napkins off the table so they could press them delicately against their sweaty brows. Surely this phenomenon would NEVER happen to me.

Fast forward thirty years, to the time my electric bills began soaring through the roof. The kids started complaining about the sub-zero temperatures inside the house, and were forced to don heavy woolen sweaters just to keep their teeth from chattering at the dinner table.

"What do you mean it's cold in the house?" I would ask them, fanning away at my face with both hands. "It feels like a damn oven in here!" I was certain that some cosmic shift had taken place, and that the earth had moved closer to the sun. My discomfort had to be the result of global warming, I was sure of it. It couldn't have a thing to do with the fact that I'd just turned fifty.

I remember my very first hot flash. I was clearing away the dishes when a hot, prickly sensation began creeping up the base of my neck. Suddenly, the heat spread down my arms and legs like wildfire, and left the palms of my hands feeling clammy. I ran over to the nearest air conditioning vent and waved my hand over it. "Honey, come quick!" I shouted. "Somebody broke the air conditioner!" My husband assured me the house was quite cool. Impossible! I checked the thermostat, and even tapped on the glass a few times in disbelief. Seventy-one degrees? The reading had to be incorrect. It felt more like ninety-five.

And just I was starting to really worry about what was happening to my internal temperature gauge, the hot sensation left my body. I once again felt cool, calm, and collected—with the exception of the beads of perspiration scattered across my forehead and upper lip. What the hell? I chalked up the whole experience to "some kind of weird body malfunction" and went about my business.

But it happened again. And again. For several months, I continued to experience unpredictable bursts of heat, and they would always occur at inconvenient or inappropriate times. Still, I remained in denial, convinced the whole world had gone completely mad—at least as far as indoor cooling systems were concerned. I adamantly refused to become one of those women who carry around a large roll of paper towels in a purse the size of a suitcase.

As bad as the days were, the nights were even worse, and sleep became nearly impossible. Sheets on, sheets off. Freezing one moment, drenched with sweat the next. Even my dreams became unpredictable. Instead of dreaming about hot guys, I dreamt about hot fudge sundaes.

At a recent party, however, I could no longer ignore the signs. After two (or was it three?) glasses of Pinot Grigio, perspiration began dripping down my skin like someone had just turned the sun up a notch and focused its rays on me through a gigantic magnifying glass. I tried discreetly to maneuver my sweaty body under the wobbly ceiling fan but somebody had beaten me to it—a woman swiping her brow with a thick layer of paper towels. I recognized the telltale signs of a female in the middle of a hot flash: flushed cheeks, limp shirt clinging to the skin, moisture trickling down her temples, and eyeliner melting down the sides of her eyelids, turning her "cat eye" into more of a "startled raccoon." She waved a paper plate in front of her face, and as we made eye contact, I knew I had met a kindred spirit.

The woman informed me that wine increased the frequency and intensity of hot flashes, which explained why she wasn't drinking anything stronger than a tumbler of ice water at the raucous party. That was the moment I should have set down my wine glass, marched into the kitchen, and wedged my head into the freezer until the hot flash disappeared. That would have been the smart thing to do. Instead, I rummaged around the kitchen cabinets until I found a fishbowl-sized glass and emptied half a bottle of wine into it. (I compensated by loading the rest of the goblet with ice.) Raising my glass, I toasted my new friends: hot flash, hot temper, and hot fudge sundae. Cheers to middle-age mamas!

Menopausal Man

SELDOM WILL YOU FIND tales of menopause that come from a man's point of view, but according to my husband, the male perspective needs to be shared. Since men have to live with us throughout the entire ordeal (remember that "for better or worse" part of the wedding vows?) and endure our hair-raising, roller-coaster ride of emotions, they deserve to be heard.

My husband strapped on his seat belt a long time ago and has ridden with me through some very rough terrain. When I was pregnant, he shared the experience with me through his own "phantom pregnancy" — as my belly expanded, so did his. If I ate Reuben sandwiches and orange sherbet for breakfast, so did he. We both craved donuts in the middle of the night, and could be found eating peanut butter straight out of the jar. When I was grouchy and crying over swollen ankles, he was miserable and swore that his ankles looked a bit swollen, too. (At least that's what he said when his socks got too tight and his jeans no longer fit. He was sure it had absolutely nothing to do with all that beer missing from the refrigerator.)

When I wasn't pregnant, and it was "that time of the month," my husband would match me in crabbiness and lower back pain. (When I found him studying the label on a bottle of Midol pills, I had to draw the line.) And now that I have crested the hill of my youth and am coasting down into the menopausal stage of life, I'll give you one guess as to who's riding behind me on the two-seater. Just the other day, I caught my husband jotting down the 1-800 number for hormone replacement therapy. I don't know if it was for his benefit or mine.

My husband and I share similar complaints about aging (weight gain, fatigue, brittle nails, creaky bones), but he has certain difficulties that I thankfully do not share. Things that only a man can understand. Like testicle issues. According to my husband, New Year's Eve in Times Square isn't the only time a ball drops. He further claims that flatulence is the bigger problem, telling me that most of the time he feels like a helium balloon avoiding a hat pin. Maybe I should just scribble "Goodyear" on his back side.

Not only has my spouse had to endure hair loss and the random appearance of skin tags, his ears have grown bigger—a phenomenon he refers to as "Dumbo Syndrome." This diagnosis makes even more sense when you consider that the patches around his sideburns have become as wrinkly as an elephant's skin. Time for him to join a herd of pachyderms.

Part of our shared moodiness and fatigue stems from lack of sleep, and I blame myself for this entirely. There is no such thing as a restful seven hours of shut-eye after one turns fifty. My husband and I refer to the new state of affairs as "the battle of the blankets," because we play tug-of-war with the sheets and bedclothes all night long. For instance, I will wake up sweating, which prompts me to use the bathroom. Once my feet hit the cold tiles, I start shivering like a leaf in a rainstorm. Meanwhile, the bed is still sizzling from my recent hot flash, which causes warmth to spread to my husband's side of the bed. Now *he's* the one having a pseudo hot flash, and just as he's kicking off the sheets, I hop back into bed, my teeth chattering, and yank three layers of covers over us. The unbearable heat wakes up my husband, who now has to take his turn stumbling bleary-eyed into the bathroom. Then, just as I'm dozing off, I hear the toilet flush and feel the familiar prickle of beads of perspiration forming across my forehead. After muttering a few choice words, I kick wildly at the blankets tangled around my legs: "Get 'em off! Get 'em OFF!"

My husband gawks at me. "Are you joking? It's freezing in here!"

To be fair, it may have taken a while, but my guy is finally start-ing to understand the mood swings of his menopausal wife. And it hasn't been an easy journey for him, particularly when you consider that sometimes it feels as if there is a loose connection between my mouth and my brain, which often causes complete insanity to roll off my tongue:

"WHO THE HELL MOVED MY CALM YOURSELF WITH YOGA BOOK THREE INCHES DOWN THE SHELF?"

"DID YOU FORGET TO BUY THE CLUMPING CAT LITTER AGAIN? I'M NOT CLEANING UP THAT #@!*#!"

"WHO ATE MY CHICKEN PARMESAN? I WAS SAVING THAT FOR MY LUNCH!"

No wonder there's been a steady increase in my husband's liquor store bill.

My spouse and kids have both learned the hard way to NEVER tell this menopausal mother to "just chill" when I'm on one of my hormonal tirades over stupid stuff like missing socks in the dryer. Two go in, one comes out. Where do they go? Mismatched sock heaven? It's these little calamities that send me over the edge. A tornado could be chewing up my backyard, but I wouldn't notice it because I'd be too busy yelling at whoever neglected to clean out the congealed macaroni-lettuce-dog-food gunk in the sink strainer.

This is what my spouse has to deal with on a regular basis—a menopausal maniac. But at least he's coming along with me for the ride.

Firebug

WHAT IS IT ABOUT men and fire? Is there an instinctive need to burn things rooted deep inside their troglodyte souls? When I was a little girl, I lived in fear that my house would burn down—which made sense, given that my brother's favorite hobby at the time was lighting matches and flicking them behind the headboard of his bed. *Why?*

During my teen years, my best friend and I were often pestered by a gas station attendant with crazy eyes and a creepy grin who gleefully referred to himself as a firebug. I kept expecting to see his face plastered all over the evening news for burning down the gas station where he worked.

Given the odds, it came as no surprise when I found myself with not one, but *two* firebugs living in my house. One of them was my youngest son, who discovered at an early age the thrill of melting a plastic truck over a hot stove and was notorious for sticking sharp objects into electrical outlets just to see the sparks fly.

The other was—my husband.

I didn't realize that my man had firebug tendencies until several years ago, during an unusually long "cold spell" in Florida (when the temperature hit a whopping sixty degrees), when our neighbor convinced us that an outdoor fire pit would be the perfect entertainment feature for our backyard garden. We agreed, and within the course of a weekend, the masterpiece was built. Just the sight of it brought warm, fuzzy visions of friends and neighbors gathering around the fire to roast marshmallows and sip hot coffee laced with brandy.

Once the fire pit was completed, my husband naturally began looking for any excuse to build a fire:

"Honey, it's Bastille Day! Time to celebrate with a fire."

"You know what would be a great way to celebrate the Summer Solstice? A fire."

"Babe, the dog didn't dig through the trash can or take a crap on the carpet! Let's have a fire!"

He also became obsessed with daily weather reports, and would check the outdoor thermometer every ten minutes to see if the mercury level had dipped below seventy degrees. (This probably explains the sudden disappearance of ice cubes from our refrigerator and the mysterious puddles beneath the thermometer.)

Those first few months spent around our fire pit were everything I had hoped for, but winter soon gave way to spring. When June arrived, I reminded my husband that it was time to dismantle the fire pit and populate the area with bright flowers. He solemnly agreed, and off he went to the nearby garden shop for a fresh batch of annuals.

An hour later he returned home with only one item. In exchange for leaving the fire pit intact so that he could continue to use it all through the boiling hot Florida summer, my husband had brought me a giant, brown misting fan that rotated and spit warm water on us. That was his compromise. Sadly, even with the fan blowing at the highest speed, our friends and I would end up sitting in a circle and perspiring like people meditating in a sweat lodge.

Unwilling to give up his obsession with fire, my husband insisted that we gather around the flames every weekend to share stories and roast marshmallows. He dubbed these evenings "Funday Sundays" and plied his guests with plenty of beer and wine so that they'd sit there, sweat, and pretend to enjoy the heat as much as he did. The smell of smoke did bring the neighbors to our backyard just as my husband had hoped, but only to make sure that our house hadn't burned down in the July heat. (What my guy didn't know was that I was secretly waving our bedroom blanket over the flames to send up a smoke signal for help.)

The problem with fires in Florida during the summer months is that no firewood is available, so we had to get creative. My husband would burn just about anything to keep his fires going—twigs, pine cones, rolls of toilet paper, credit card statements, and once, out of desperation, a box of feminine products from under my daughter's sink. It wasn't long before our neighbors began scratching their heads in bewilderment because they couldn't figure out what was happening to all of their lovely shade trees.

Another strategy my husband would use whenever firewood was sparse was to call our nephew (a.k.a. "the Mountain Man"), a survivalist who could easily beat the competition on any reality television survival show. I swear this man carries an axe in one pocket and a machete in the other—he learned at an early age to always be prepared. My nephew has an uncanny ability to sniff out wood, and can spot it as easily as a hawk circling its prey. He and my husband would become a little giddy after the holidays were over because of the abundance of discarded Christmas trees just waiting to be burned.

I'll admit there was something soothing and intimate about sitting in the darkness with the crackle and pop of a fire. We huddled closer, shared secrets, and sometimes broke out into rounds of "Row, Row, Row Your Boat." But before winter hits again, I've come up with some new rules about fire pit etiquette for my husband:

1. There will be no consumption of beans one hour before sitting around the fire. Anyone who has seen the movie *Blazing Saddles* knows why this rule must be strictly enforced.

2. My husband may not burn foreign objects in the fire, such as: the baby's dirty diapers, the leftover "Fiesta Surprise" casserole, the kitchen garbage that someone was too lazy to drag out to the curb, and the hidden receipts from Donut World, Chocolate

World, and Wine Around the World. Large pieces of cardboard should be outlawed as well, since they lift up in a draft and hover like fiery bats from hell before flapping their way toward my hair.

3. My last and favorite rule, however, is the one my nephew The Mountain Man came up with, and I think the reasons are obvious: "WHAT HAPPENS AT THE FIRE PIT, STAYS AT THE FIRE PIT!"

Wild Child

THERE'S ONE IN EVERY FAMILY: the Wild Child. The one who gives you gray hairs, anxiety weight, and over-sized baggage under the eyes. The one who breaks your heart, then turns around and mends it with his unconditional love. The one you stare at while scratching your head and saying, "Are you my child, or was I impregnated by an alien during a UFO abduction that I just can't recall?"

My youngest son is our family's Wild Child. He pulled his very first prank on the family when he made his appearance into this world several weeks early, causing my water to break on my way to volunteer at the elementary school.

To be fair, he wasn't always troublesome. He was a sweet baby — until the point he became mobile. Overnight, my little guy became almost superhuman. There wasn't a door or toddler gate my Baby Terminator couldn't conquer; there were no forbidden objects he couldn't reach. My reigning title as "The Good Mother" quickly gave way to my Native American name "She Who Drinks and Swears a Lot."

My son never played with normal children's toys — he liked sticking sharp objects into electrical outlets instead. He was like a drug-sniffing dog when it came to finding knives, poisonous bug repellents, and exposed wires. I knew I had a problem when he'd stick something into a socket, and then giggle over the little jolts of electricity running through his body. My son was like a cat with nine lives, and he had no fear of losing a few of them to satisfy his dangerous curiosity.

He also had a quick temper. It simmered beneath his calm exterior until he would strike like a cobra at his unsuspecting victims. No one was safe from the objects my miniature Hulk could hurl across a room—irons, dictionaries, toasters, one time even a large Barbie car. I thought for certain his three older siblings would kill him before he saw his third birthday.

When my son turned four, we took him on his first trip to Disney World, along with my parents, my older siblings, and their families. This was my big chance to demonstrate my "awesome" parenting skills in front of my folks, and as every mother knows, this is an opportunity not to be wasted. For the most part, my children's behavior was excellent—until we visited Magic Kingdom and all hell broke loose.

While my husband took the older kids on some of the faster rides, I stayed behind with my little boy and his grandparents. Within minutes, I noticed that my son was chewing away on a large blob of bubble gum—that I hadn't given him. I never gave my children gum, and I became instantly ready to do battle with whatever family member had felt it wise to give a wad of gum the size of a golf ball to a four-year-old. But when I asked him where he'd gotten it, he pointed to a green pole near the "It's a Small World" ride.

The minute my son saw the horror register on my face, he snapped his mouth shut, and the gum became sealed behind lips closed tighter than the doors at Fort Knox.

It was the beginning of the end of my reign as "Most Awesome Parent." My folks had to help hold down their flailing, screaming grandchild, while I came just short of using the Jaws of Life to pry open my son's mouth and retrieve the gum that someone else in the park had previously enjoyed. Convinced he was going to contract some fatal disease, I had to fight back an overwhelming urge to wash the germs out of his mouth with antibacterial soap.

While the Disney World gum incident may have been the first of its kind, there were many incidents like it that followed, and there were not enough parenting manuals in the world to teach me how to handle a kid who risked his life on a daily basis. His interest in matches, electricity, and the dismantling of anything that wasn't nailed to the floor was enough to convince me this child could never, EVER be left alone. Even with constant supervision he managed to dislocate his shoulder, fracture his wrist, and bring a knife to elementary school. (I must have missed the memo in which my husband announced his BRILLIANT intentions to give our little boy a camping knife.)

During the god-awful middle school years, my son wore low-slung "gangsta" jeans with torn, disgusting hems that dragged all over the ground. I threatened to burn those pants so many times— while he was still in them. Late to class one morning, while he was running to beat the bell, he tripped over those damned jeans, and off we went to the hospital to have a metal screw put into his damaged hip bone. Needless to say, his wardrobe only consisted of shorts after *that* hefty medical bill.

One of the worst incidents I can remember was when my four-teen-year-old son decided to run away from home rather than deal with the consequences of a poor report card. The world stopped that afternoon when he didn't return home from school. I was trapped in every parent's worst nightmare; my child had disappeared without a trace. It wasn't long before police began swarming our street and patrolling the surrounding neighborhoods in search of my boy.

After spending several torturous hours pacing, crying, and begging God to bring my son home safely, the police found him on a Greyhound Bus headed for Orlando. It was a miracle he survived the trip unscathed. A wave of relief washed over me—followed by an understandable wave of anger. I could feel the hairs on my head turning whiter by the second.

After that fretful day, my husband and I started to make major changes in our son's life in order to help improve his behavior and attitude. He discovered drums, bodybuilding, and biking, which are his passions now and provide him safe, productive ways to be himself. His sense of humor and enthusiasm is often what gets me through the day, and I'm proud to say he's as strong as an ox and very protective of his mother.

Despite all of our efforts, though, my son is still pushing the envelope on his nine lives. A few months after the Greyhound incident, he was injured in a biking accident after colliding with another cyclist. Shortly after that, he was hit by a car while biking down to the beach. Interestingly enough, the car suffered more damage than my son—it was no match for my Schwarzenegger-esque offspring.

It was this next incident, however, that threatened to send me into permanent cardiac arrest. Another one of my husband's genius ideas had been to give our boy a special pellet gun that looked exactly like an AK-47. My son was out front shooting targets on the sidewalk—probably not the smartest idea since we live only a few doors down from a school—when suddenly my peaceful afternoon was shattered by the sound of screeching tires and a loud voice booming over a megaphone: "DROP THE GUN AND PUT YOUR HANDS UP IN THE AIR!" Our street was soon barricaded by four police cars and six officers, one of them with a gun drawn on my son.

I stood by my front window, frozen in horror, as I watched my boy slowly lower the gun and walk backwards down the sidewalk, his hands held high in the air. In a flash, one of the officers snapped handcuffs on his wrists. There was a brief moment when my eyes met my son's, and I could see the fear and bewilderment in his gaze. I couldn't move—my legs felt like wet noodles—but thankfully my husband rushed out the door to explain that my son's deadly weapon was just a pellet gun, not an assault rifle.

I never know what my boy will think up next to keep himself entertained, which is why I shudder every time he climbs into a car and drives off with his friends. Nevertheless, while he is often the typical, unpredictable, and annoying Wild Child teenager, he is also loyal, loving, artistic, and compassionate. Even better, he knows how to operate the lawn mower, vacuum, dishwasher, washing machine, and grill. His uniqueness is what makes him one of the most fascinating people I know, and I'm proud to call him my son.

But by my calculations, he hasn't used up all nine lives, so I'm still sprouting gray hairs.

Six Good Things About Raising Teenage Boys

I HAVE FOUR CHILDREN, three of whom are now adults and have (thankfully) flown the coop—which is why I started to let myself think I had this whole "raising teenagers" thing down. I may have even given myself a hearty. pat on the back for getting the first three off to college without any arrest records or shotgun weddings.

And then came number four, who could easily be the poster child for birth control.

As I've mentioned, this boy is the reason why I go through an industrial-size bucket of hair dye every month, and why I've been a gold-card-carrying member of our local Wine Mart for almost twenty years. A typical morning with this kid involves matches, an aerosol can of cologne spray, a plastic milk jug, and a shrieking fire alarm—all before my coffee has kicked in.

Despite the heart palpitations that plague me daily as a result of my son's wild and crazy behavior, I've nonetheless discovered that there are many positive aspects to raising a teenage boy:

1. You no longer need to waste money on expensive theme parks with fast rides. Your teen will gladly attach your rolling office

chair to his bike with a rope and pull his buddies down a busy highway. Like a heart-stopping adrenaline rush? Then having a teenage boy is for you.

2. Piss-yellow will become your favorite shade of bathroom tile, because there isn't enough Clorox in the world to make those urine stains around the toilet disappear. Fortunately for you, piss-yellow bathroom tile is *always* on sale.

3. Like pets? You're in luck, because small critters will migrate to your home just to nest in the sour-smelling pile of laundry at the back of your son's closet. Dirty dishes and half-eaten cheese sticks will also entice armies of cockroaches to build vacation homes under his bed.

4. If you failed science in high school, don't worry. You're going to get a hands-on education in fire mitigation, the dangers of electricity, and just how much damage a potato bomb can do to your neighbor's fence.

5. You'll finally lose those last stubborn ten pounds, since all boys are born with noses like bloodhounds. They sniff out every hidden cookie, potato chip, and Mother's Day chocolate, even the ones you tried to hide in an empty Summer's Eve box under the bathroom sink. Your grocery bill may triple during his teen years, but believe me, your waistline will shrink. Just be sure to lock the liquor cabinet before he turns fifteen.

6. Miss those nights of club-hopping while you were in your twenties? You can relive your youth every time your teenage boy hosts a rave in his bedroom, blasting techno and dubstep from subwoofers the size of refrigerators. Toss back some tequila shots chased by a few aspirin and you'll feel like you've time-traveled back to a good ol' fashioned warehouse party.

Even though there will be days when you'll wish you could lobotomize your son, or trade him in for a house-trained Labrador, just remember how much fun it'll be when he has sons of his own. Grab a lighter and load up the potato gun. Karma has a sense of humor, after all.

Nine Signs You Might Be a MILF

DOES YOUR TEENAGE son have a friend who prefers to lounge on the sofa with you while all the other boys are outside playing baseball? Does your daughter's boyfriend find every possible excuse to come in for a quick hug, or a peck on the cheek? Are the boys in the neighborhood suspiciously nice to you while showing a complete disregard for every other mom they know? If you answered yes to any or all of these questions, you might just be a MILF.

I had no idea what the term MILF meant until 1999, when my high-school-aged kids convinced me to watch the teen movie and box office hit *American Pie*. The movie was rife with the ridiculous shenanigans of an apple-pie-humping teenager and his circle of friends; needless to say, I found the film to be a highly educational experience.

While my kids were in high school, our family encouraged a revolving-door policy when it came to the teens in the neighborhood, so our home was always full of young people. Whenever male guests would linger a little too long beside me, all of the other kids would snicker and accuse me of being a MILF. Although I found the label disturbing, I'll admit I was just a teensy bit flattered that an eighteen-year-old would be attracted to my fortyish self.

Sorry, but it's true.

If you're raising teens, and wondering whether or not you're a MILF, watch for these classic signs the next time the teenage boys come calling:

1. They prefer hanging out in the kitchen with you rather than playing the latest video game with your son. Don't be fooled by their sudden interest in your onion-dicing technique. And, for God's sake, leave the cucumbers in the refrigerator.

2. They'll tell you how pretty you look even when you're wearing a ratty housedress and fluffy leopard-print slippers. Right, guys? Because nothing screams "sexy" more than a middle-aged mama rocking curlers and a pasty-green botanicals masque.

3. They arrive at your doorstep in freshly pressed shirts, reeking of AXE body spray.

4. Whatever odd job you might have for them, they'll jump at the chance to do it—whether it be washing your car, plunging your toilet, or pulling hairballs out of your shower drain.

5. They'll call or stop by the house even when they know your kids aren't home. Learn to recognize this for what it is—an excuse to engage you in awkward conversations about their girlfriend problems and love lives.

6. They'd much rather watch vintage black-and-white movies with you than hit the basketball court with their friends.

7. No matter what you cook, they'll compliment your culinary skills, and swear your food tastes better than anything their own mothers could *ever* make—even when you're serving them freezer-burned fish sticks nuked way too long in the microwave.

8. They'll use any pretext to make physical contact. A popular choice is the "comfort hug," in which they offer you solace for any ridiculous tragedy they can think up, such as a painful-looking hangnail or the dead goldfish you just flushed down the toilet.

9. They'll friend you on Facebook and leave flirty comments all over your status updates, including the one you wrote about neutering the cat.

My MILF days are probably behind me, but you know what? It's not the end of the world. Now that I'm a first-time grandmother, I've been promoted to GILF! Warm apple pie, anyone?

Welcome to the Jungle

IT STARTED WITH the hamsters. The minute my daughters saw the fuzzy little rodents at the pet store, they started begging me to buy them. Against my better judgment, I agreed, and we left the store that day with a deluxe critter condo equipped with tunnels, chew toys, and a fancy exercise wheel to keep our new pets in perfect hamster form. Little did we know that these furry, nocturnal nightmares would take their exercise in the middle of the night, running for hours on that squeaky wheel like toddlers hyped up on Kool-Aid.

We also discovered that hamsters breed much faster than their rabbit relatives. When Mama Hamster gave birth to nine babies and ate three for lunch, my daughters learned a valuable lesson in parenting: never cross your mother when she's having a bad day.

Hamsters were only the beginning of our family's adventures in animal hoarding. There were turtles that caused my son's bedroom to smell like rancid swampland. There was a long-haired guinea pig that looked like a misguided hippie from the era of peace and love. And yet who knew guinea pigs had such sharp teeth?

Our home quickly earned the reputation of being a modern day Noah's Ark, and we were soon inundated with enough homeless animals to start a petting zoo. At one point, we fostered two albino rats, a hedgehog, a sugar glider, and seven chinchillas. The day I brought home a stray rabbit, my husband protested loudly over my inability to turn down any creature covered in fur. He was certain that one day he'd come home to find Sasquatch sitting at our dinner table.

In addition to our smorgasbord of exotic pets, we also own three rescue dogs. One is on heart medication, the other is losing all of his hair, and the third wears a diaper—it's like we're running a canine convalescent home. The diaper-wearing dog is a pug with the appetite of a goat and a digestive system that functions like a recycling plant. We make his diapers by hand from feminine hygiene pads. Unfortunately, he often eats the pads and then poops out tampons.

Besides being messy, our animal collection has also been a source of family drama. When my children were teenagers, they accused me of loving our animals more than I loved them. (This was a no-brainer for me since the animals never talked back.) My husband also grew suspicious when he noticed hordes of squirrels colonizing in our trees, and I'll admit that the daily buffet of peanuts and seeds I'd been feeding them was costing enough to support a third world country. I've also been banned from visiting the zoo or even watching *Animal Planet*, for fear that I'll bring home a family of penguins or jackalopes.

I don't think I'll tell my family that lately I've been googling BOGO sales on Kinkajous. My husband has already threatened to enroll me in a ten-step program at Animal Hoarders Anonymous if I don't stop. He'd much prefer I collect Hummel figurines or enroll in some knitting classes.

Which I've agreed to do—at the yarn shop right next to the pet store.

Queen of Klutz

MY INJURED HAND throbs as I sit in the emergency clinic and wait to have it stitched up. It had been such a perfect day—how had I ended up *here*? Ah, that's right. A treacherous combination of baby gates, sleeping dogs, and glass coffee mugs—and the fact that I'm a klutz.

I'm rarely sick or injured, but when I do catch the latest bug or become the victim of my own awkwardness, I tend to go all out. There is no middle ground for me when it comes to injury or disease; I'm either perfectly fine or a walking disaster. When I was a little kid, for example, I decided to pester our family German shepherd while he was eating—and he mistook my face for a pork chop. Four stitches just below the eye taught me never to come between a dog and his Alpo again.

On the eve of an important high school band competition, a scary-looking spider bit me on the arm. It stung like hell, but I knew if I told my parents, they would never let me go to the out-of-town competition—so I kept my mouth shut. The next morning, the bus driver had to stop at least a dozen times so that I could ralph on the side of the road. All dignity was lost at that point, but for once I didn't care how green or disheveled I looked to the others on the bus. My arm was on fire. All I could think about was finishing the competition and heading home.

When the contest ended later that day, I pulled back my sleeve to reveal angry, red tracks drag racing up my arm toward my heart. "Excuse me. Is there a doctor in the house?" The green infection that the doctor drained from my arm looked like something an alien would spew after eating genetically modified foods.

My freshman year of college, I decided to get sporty (or at least fake it) and invite my roommate to play Frisbee on the front lawn of our dorm. I'm about as athletic as an elephant on the U.S. Olympic Swim Team, but I had an ulterior motive—to attract the attention of some University of Missouri males who were strolling across our campus. It was all fun and games until my friend tackled me for the Frisbee and fell hard on my left arm, snapping both bones in half. Shock set in when I saw the middle of my arm curve into a backward "L," like some funky-shaped piece of pasta. A metal plate, five screws, and one pin later, I had a bionic arm that would set off alarms at airports for a long time to come.

Fast forward two years—same college, different friends—to the time I slipped down a flight of icy stairs and busted my ankle. Back to the same hospital, where I was outfitted with a very stylish cast and a complimentary set of crutches. (My fall had absolutely nothing to do with the "hunch punch" served at a certain sorority party, of course. I'd just figured I would start a new fashion trend at the spring formal—because nothing speaks sexy more than a college co-ed hobbling through a line dance with a cast on her leg.)

A few months after graduation, I ended up in that very same ER for the third time in four years, after taking a tumble in a parking lot and fracturing my elbow. By that point, I was on a first-name basis with the nurses, and I had all of the doctors' business cards in my Rolodex.

Things were quiet for several years until I thought it might be fun to experience labor pains. My mother had popped out babies faster than bubbles out of a bubble blower, so I assumed it would be the same for me. WRONG. Four kids and four C-sections later, I am the proud owner of a belly that looks like I have a road map to "The Land Down Under" tattooed onto my skin.

And then there was the infamous *Night of the Living Dead* experience. Imagine a romantic anniversary celebration at a fancy resort, complete with candles, flowers, champagne, and a wife with her head in the toilet, yacking up chicken chop suey and imported Italian chocolates. I even had a creepy, out-of-body experience, where I gazed down and saw myself curled into the fetal position (bearing an uncanny resemblance to a gray, uncooked shrimp) on the bathroom tile. The paramedics arrived just in time to pump my body with hydrating fluids and cart me off to the nearest hospital.

You know the part in your wedding vows where you SWEAR you'll stick by your spouse through sickness and in health? I gave that vow a run for its money that night. What wasn't coming out of my mouth was shooting out the other end. Even the nurses refused to come in contact with me, since the doctors were unable to identify what virus I had. I knew it was bad when the staff came in with masks on their faces to spray my area with disinfectant. During all this, my husband never left my side, taking on the job of cleaning me up when no one else would. That, folks, is someone who takes his vows seriously.

And now, as I leave the emergency clinic with eight stitches, I wish I could tell you that the nasty condition of my zombie-looking hand is due to something sensational, like a bare-knuckle boxing match or a rowdy bar fight. And I wish I could tell you that the other guy's face looks much worse than my hand. Sadly, my accident can only be blamed on my klutziness. I should have known that hopping over a baby gate with a glass coffee mug in my hand, all while trying to avoid two sleeping pugs, was a recipe for disaster. (I keep reminding myself that I'm long past the age of twenty and not nearly as agile—but obviously I ignore my own words of wisdom.) Needless to say, my toe caught on the gate and I tripped and fell into the kitchen, landing in the shards of glass from the broken mug. I never realized how badly a hand injury bled, until I noticed that my kitchen looked like the inside of a slaughterhouse.

As the doctor stitched me up, he apologized for the scar it would leave. I laughed and showed him all my others. The way I see it, each one carries with it a new story to share with the grandkids someday. And in typical writer fashion, I took pictures of my bloody, stitched-up hand for the story that was already taking shape in my head.

When we left the emergency clinic, I told my husband that I thought I deserved chocolate for my ordeal. He smirked and said that at my age, what I REALLY needed was a Life Alert necklace.

Sleepus Interruptus

I LOVE MY QUIET WEEKENDS. They give me license to indulge in one of my favorite pastimes—napping. When the lunch dishes are cleared and my schedule is free, I retire to my private little paradise under a stack of blankets and pillows. Once I close my bedroom door, the family KNOWS not to disturb me. They understand all too well that if my beauty rest is interrupted, they'll be dealing with a haggard ogre, and the consequences for waking me will be swift and painful.

Most weekends I can steal a little shut-eye by midafternoon. I'm a firm believer in a three-hour siesta. But lately, uncontrollable outside forces have been messing with the sweet slumber I so desperately crave. No, I'm not referring to young children screeching or running through the house. What I'm referring to are things like the obnoxious neighborhood ice cream truck that takes sadistic pleasure in blaring "Pop Goes the Weasel" from massive speakers as it drives repeatedly past my home. The driver's timing is always precise—just as I am in the throes of a deliciously sexy dream, about to lock lips with George Clooney: POP GOES THE WEASEL!

At times like this, I grit my teeth against the sudden urge for an orange Creamsicle, burrow deeper under the covers, and wait for the offending truck to pass. Just when I start to slip back into the land of Nod, the doorbell rings and the dogs go insane. Over their incessant barking, a salesman tries to convince me that I need to switch cable companies and add an additional 500 channels to the existing 700 I already have. Hey, I never get the chance to sleep, so why not have even more opportunities to live vicariously through the people testing out Tempur-Pedic mattresses on late-night infomercials?

The salesman leaves, and I finally get the chance to drift back into the slumber I have been looking forward to all week. I never know how much time passes—it could be two hours or two minutes—but inevitably, the next-door neighbor who won last year's Curb Appeal Award will decide to do a little creative landscaping. As he trims the base of his perfectly squared hedge with a weed-whacker, small stones ricochet loudly off my bedroom window. It sounds like a woodpecker on steroids. I'd rather sleep in a room filled with chocolate-wasted toddlers than listen to the torturous cacophony of flying debris from my neighbor's new lawn toy.

I decide to give napping one more shot when suddenly I find myself baking in a four hundred and seventy-five degree oven. Who invited the freaking sun into my bedroom? Within seconds, I'm bathed in a puddle of sweat and riding out the aftershocks of a merciless hot flash.

Giving up on the fantasy of a three-hour nap, I stagger into the kitchen for a jolt of caffeine to push me through the rest of the day. Peering around the corner, I see my husband sleeping peacefully on the couch, his lips puffing out with each whistling exhale. I hear the TV in the background—a testosterone-infused program on cage fighting—and marvel at his ability to sleep through doorbells, barking dogs, and men locked in combat. Actually, I'm a wee bit jealous. Okay, a LOT jealous.

Deciding that it really wouldn't be fair for my well-rested husband to be stuck with a wife who resembles a troll, I wake him from sleep. He opens one eye, peers up at me, and smiles. I hand him a cup of coffee and flop down beside him on the couch. He channel surfs like a kid with severe ADD before settling on the Discovery Channel. Grinning, he wraps his arms around me, and I snuggle against his warmth. Within minutes, I drift into blessed slumber.

I can't think of a better way to spend a Sunday afternoon than nodding off during a television documentary about the sleeping habits of wombats, while curled in the arms of the man I love.

Born This Way

MY DAY STARTS LONG before the sun comes up.

Like many other women my age, I'm often up all night with insomnia. When this happens, stupid stuff swirls around in my sleepless brain like scraps of paper in a wind storm. Did I turn the stove off after dinner? Are the garbage can lids fastened securely enough to keep stray dogs out of the trash? Did I remember to pay my out-of-control water bill? Why the hell did I eat that last meatball? I didn't need it or want it, but it was just sitting there by its lonesome self on the plate, calling my name.

On these sleepless nights, I usually give up on trying to sleep around 5:30 a.m., and start slowly shuffling through the house like a disgruntled zombie. After drinking mass quantities of caffeine, the sun seems not quite as offensive, so I hit the walking trail for a few laps. It's my hope that the exercise will wake me up and make me feel better, but when I get back home, my legs ache like crazy and my skin is positively raw under the bra line. Why? Because I'm chafed. Chafed! I'm too young to chafe! Even if it *is* 100 percent humidity and ninety-five degrees outside.

The pain and indignity of my soreness and chafing starts me down an unhappy trail of self-consciousness. It's not the first time. An overall lack of sleep and low levels of estrogen have been causing my inner wiring to fritz out, and lately my behavior has become erratic. Yesterday I cried over a Humana commercial. Today I'm obsessed with Hershey's Kisses. Last week I went nuts because there were no clean towels left and I couldn't take a shower.

I can feel myself cresting another wicked mood swing, and I have no idea how long it will last. I hear my daughter whisper to her younger brother, "Don't bug Mom today. She's in her dark place," and I know it's time for me to retire to my bat cave and ponder the meaning of life. Alone. I stay there for as long as it takes to get a hold of myself.

After brooding in my cave for an hour, I decide to once again join the land of the living. I hear music drifting down the hall—Lady Gaga's "Born This Way." Born what way? Born to chafe and sneak Hershey's Kisses out of the pantry? God, I hope not. I want to start over in a world where menopause does not exist—or at least has an entirely different meaning, such as "pause for a vacation," "pause for a Mai Tai," or "pause for a romp with my husband." Anything but what has culminated into a perspiring woman in an "I'm Nuts for Squirrels" T-shirt, fanning herself with a pink dust pan.

The kids scatter like frightened mice as I make my way out into the living room. My husband eyes me warily from the couch and quickly flips the channel to something a little more soothing than MMA cage wrestling—like polar bears circling a seal. I appreciate his efforts, but I'm starting to think that right now the world under my comforter looks a whole lot better.

Yeah, I know what you're thinking. I'm a conglomeration of Snow White's dwarfs: Grumpy, Sleepy, Sneezy, Bitchy, Bloaty, Sweaty, and Weepy. Hey, don't judge. Baby, I was born this way.

A Letter to My Younger Self

YOU PROBABLY DON'T recognize me with these little lines around my eyes, and a figure that's gone south after giving birth to four children. But there's nothing to be ashamed of here. These lines by my eyes come from years of laughter, and the scars on my belly are a badge of motherhood that I wear with pride. I've learned so much over the course of this crazy, happy existence, and I want to share with you what life's many ups and downs have taught me.

When you get into high school, don't worry so much about what other people think. Just be who you want to be, not what your peers expect you to be. Embrace your individuality—it will be the ticket to your success one day.

Although your teenage years may feel like nothing more than a popularity contest, in the end you'll be happier sticking with a small circle of friends who love you for who you are. They'll be the ones holding the catcher's mitts when life starts throwing you its inevitable curve balls.

Forgiveness. I know this is a tough one for you, but trust me when I say that bitterness will only weigh you down. Let go of the anger you feel toward those kids who poke fun at you—what you don't realize is how unkind their lives are. Their spirits have been broken and they've learned the hard way that they can protect themselves by preying on vulnerable people like you. Don't allow them to make you feel stupid and small inside.

You waste too much energy berating yourself in front of the mirror. Society has fed you a warped perception of beauty—don't let it convince you that you fall short of everyone else's expectations. Stop punishing yourself with starvation diets, and quit binge eating to mask what's really bothering you. I know how much you're hurting; you just haven't yet figured out that inner beauty outlives physical beauty every time. See yourself through your own eyes, and know that others love you, even when you don't love yourself.

You will suffer some unimaginable losses in the years to come— don't be afraid to face them head on. You're going to walk through a valley of grief, but you're going to come out the other side a stronger, braver woman. You'll need these experiences so that you can hold up *your* loved ones when life knocks them down.

I know you feel as though your parents are judging every move you make, and I know you hate living under a microscope. Strict curfews, suspended phone privileges, and being grounded from social activities may all seem unreasonable now, but your parents really do have your best interests at heart. If they didn't love you, they wouldn't care what you did. Boundaries and rules are a sign of good parenting and tough love. You'll figure this out once you have kids of your own.

Don't be in such a hurry to grow up. Slow down and enjoy the ride. Even though you're struggling with some tough, emotional issues, each experience is a small piece of the larger puzzle—the composition of the beautiful person you'll become. Every day should be your happiest. Live life to the fullest. It will never be this way again.

Appreciate the time you have with your family. Those summer vacations won't last forever. Take your father on that trip to Scotland before it's too late, and spend more time hanging out with your sister. Don't assume she'll always be there for you, because she won't. She'll be gone sooner than you think, and her absence will leave a void in your life that cannot be filled by anyone else.

You're going to fall in love several times while you're young, but be very conscious of the men you choose. Your happiness shouldn't depend on them. One will break your heart and in the process, break his own. Others will come and go, but each one will teach you a valuable lesson in love that will help prepare you for the man you're going to marry. Stay away from the sly one at the bar who asks you to dance. Nothing good will come from this. His lies will hurt you more than his fists. He'll tear you down to keep you from standing back up, but in time, you will. You are a survivor. One day you'll meet your soul mate, and he'll help you find your smile again.

Life is full of twists and turns—don't be afraid to stray from the well-worn path that everyone else is walking. Embrace the challenges you'll face and don't let the fear of failure box you into years of regret. How will you ever learn anything if you never make a mistake? Trust your intuition, listen to your heart, and fight hard for what you believe. Stop wasting precious time running down hollow streets in search of happiness. You'll soon find that it's been inside you all along.

The Vulture Years

MY DAUGHTER ONCE convinced me to watch a cable reality show about models. As I stared in disbelief at the slew of twenty-one-year-old women gracing the screen, I wondered—was I ever that young? I felt more like something an anthropologist had just unearthed from King Tut's tomb.

My brain is convinced that I'm still twenty-five, but my body has fast-forwarded into a new century populated by people with graying hair, pot bellies, and saggy skin. Is this really the generation I was born into? What happened to red leather pants and Boy George? If people had told me thirty years ago that I'd be spending my weekends in the backyard using a pooper scooper, I would have laughed in their faces. My husband feels the same way every time he gets behind the wheel of our prehistoric minivan—the one that should have been shot and put out of its misery years ago.

For the most part, I'm young at heart. Some days, however, I feel like it's time for the kids to wheel me into a nursing home and start spoon-feeding me soup. I'm already getting flyers in the mail pestering me to shop for burial plots and take tours of local retirement centers. Just the other day, I was on the walking trail with my husband when I noticed a vulture circling overhead. It followed us for a mile or two, as if waiting to see which one would croak first. My husband raised his fist to the bird and shouted, "We're not dead yet!"

I never had age spots on my skin. Then suddenly, I woke up one morning looking like a leopard. I rushed over to the dermatologist, convinced that I had some sort of skin disease. She chuckled and said, "Welcome to middle age!" Now the spots are all over me— enough that if I'm bored, I can play connect-the-dots on my skin. Some dots are lighter and some darker; some are smaller and others larger. Some are the size of Africa. By the time I'm eighty, I'll be one giant, brown age spot. On the plus side, I'll have a great tan without even trying.

My eyes have also gone to hell. My mother promised me when I was little that if I ate my carrots, I'd have good eyesight. She lied. I'm blinder than the love child of a bat and mole.

I now depend on certain "senior accessories" to get me through each day: a gallon jug of skin cream (heavy on the SPF, of course), Benefiber, aspirin, lip balm, ear plugs, nose spray, padded shoe inserts, reading glasses, a knee brace and my mouth guard for night-time. I suppose I could throw in a tube of Icy Hot, a bottle of B-12 pills, a pair of support hose, and some high-heeled orthopedic shoes to make my life more interesting. What better time to embrace the vulture years?

The Truth About Aging

I RECENTLY ACCOMPANIED my mother to a Life Line Screening appointment, so that we could have our hearts and arteries checked. We do this annually due to a family history of aortic aneurysms. Glancing around the crowded waiting room, I realized there were no other patients under the age of seventy, which made me the youngest whippersnapper in the group. It was a nice feeling, since I'm usually the old fart at social engagements.

After my mother filled out all the necessary forms, she gave me "the talk." No, not THAT talk. There would be something seriously wrong with me if I hadn't figured out by now where my four babies had come from. No, Mom just wanted me to know that there is more to aging than the usual symptoms people complain about—more personal "stuff" that no one but a mother would feel comfortable sharing with me.

Since I'm way past *What to Expect When You're Expecting*, I was very interested in what sage advice my mother wanted to impart. Imagine my surprise when she gave me a condensed version of her *own* handbook—*What to Expect When You're Expecting Rigor Mortis*.

She told me:

- Your teeth will shift, costing you a small fortune in dental floss and toothpicks. Your gums will also recede, so much so that your teeth will be twice the size they used to be. Forget eating beef—if you do, you'll be digging an entire cow out of your molars by the time dinner is over.

- Certain muscles in the body will thin out and relax to the point where you'll once again be forced to troll the feminine products aisle at the grocery store. The only difference is that this time you'll be filling your cart with Poise and Depends instead of Kotex and Tampax.
- Spandex will no longer hold in your avalanche of sagging skin. Time for a full-body girdle.
- Lifting yourself up from the couch will fulfill your daily exercise requirements.
- Gas will strike at inopportune moments, like weddings and funerals. Remember the old days, when you used to be able to clear a dance floor with your disco moves? Now you'll clear a room with your flatulence. After the age of sixty, you'll have the equivalent of a putt-putt motor strapped to your butt, with no control over when it will activate.
- Your eyesight will steadily decrease, to the point where you'll need glasses with the magnifying power of the Hubble Telescope.
- Hearing loss will be unavoidable. Your family will become so annoyed with the amount of times you ask "Huh?" and "What?" that you'll end up scouring eBay for an affordable ear trumpet. Basically, you'll hear very little—unless, of course, someone is offering you cake. Then you'll hear just fine.
- You'll shop for comfort rather than for style or sex appeal. Your closets and drawers will be overflowing with embroidered sweaters, side-snap pants, and compression hose.
- Osteoporosis will become a real issue. Your bones will be fragile, and you'll bruise faster than a banana. Pretty soon you'll need to invest in hockey goalie gear, so that you'll be safely padded against possible fractures.
- Despite spending a small fortune on facial serums and creams with a higher SPF than your IQ, you'll be unable to prevent laugh lines from forming deep ravines in your skin. You will

live in fear of ending up with a face that resembles the shriveled-up peach in the back of your refrigerator's produce drawer.

- Your boobs and your butt will be in a race to reach your ankles.
- Your sex drive will drop considerably. Forget spending your golden years learning the art of tantric sex with your partner—the only thing happening in bed will be the missionary position and your spouse asking "Are you still awake?" halfway through.
- Memory loss will be great fun if you don't mind playing hide-and-seek with your personal items.
- A Hoveround electric mobility chair will look more appealing than a flashy sports car.
- Unexplained aches and pains will become the norm. Arthritis will cause you to pop ibuprofen like candy. By the end of each day, your body will feel like it has been through a rousing game of Whac-A-Mole.
- When you visit the caveman section of the museum, you'll feel right at home.

After hearing my mother's words of wisdom, a nurse called our names. As I slipped out of the chair with ease, I realized that I should appreciate every day I have before needing to trade in my wine for Geritol. Unless, of course, wine turns out to be water from the Fountain of Youth. If that's the case, I'll be young forever.

Keep Your Eggs Out of My Empty Nest

THERE WAS A TIME when I took pride in the fact that my house was one of the busiest (and noisiest) on the street. In addition to my own four children, I took care of five others during the after-school hours, and the rest of the neighborhood kids were welcome to come over whenever they chose.

On one particular rainy afternoon, I counted seventeen kids—ranging in age from ten to seventeen—in my matchbox-sized home. I'm convinced this was when my love for margaritas began.

My house was always LOUD. Music blasting, televisions blaring, children giggling and squealing, and plenty of unruly games of basketball in the driveway—these things were the norm. The chaos never bothered me. I loved my role as the entertaining, "cool" mom, and was happy to provide enough calorie-laden snacks to feed an Army brigade.

Three of my four children are now grown. The last one at home is in high school, so he'd rather have a root canal than spend an evening with dear old Mom and Dad. This allows us quite a bit of wiggle room as far as privacy is concerned, as well as a glimpse of what life will be like when my youngest packs his bags and heads off to college (hopefully to a school on the other side of the continent). I already know I'm going to LOVE being an empty nester.

With just the two of us, we'll enjoy a reduced grocery bill. My monthly supermarket expenses will finally be lower than my mortgage payment. I'll no longer need to fill every available space in my home with toilet paper, gallons of milk, and cases of AXE body spray. My house will also stay clean—no more unmade beds, sloppy rooms, or restrooms requiring weekly bleach baths. And cooking will become a joy once again, if only because I won't be catering for a crowd every night. My husband and I will be perfectly content to snarf down bowls of cereal for dinner while watching an episode of *Hoarders*.

With an empty house, my man and I will also have the chance to rekindle the passion we had in our twenties. Sex all day, every day? Maybe. At the very least, each night can be a date night, with the potential for any moment to become a Cialis moment. The only thing missing? Matching bathtubs in wildly inappropriate places, like the tool aisle at Sears.

We'll finally be able to have a REAL adult conversation again instead of the usual parent platitudes:

"Has he pooped today?"

"Make sure he brushes his teeth before bed."

"Does she want fries with that?"

We'll also have the freedom to take spontaneous excursions anywhere we want in the world—or maybe just to Kmart—without needing to hire a babysitter.

No kiddie school means no more math homework ($Y=mx+b$ ... HUH?), no more erupting science-project volcanoes in the kitchen, and no more thirty-page term papers causing tears of frustration— from Mom. No more school also means no more expensive school uniforms, and more importantly, no more school supplies. "What do you mean you need a specific brand of environmentally-safe markers made in China by three-fingered panda bears?"

Furthermore, as an empty nester, I can finally quit my part-time job as taxi driver, shuttling kids to and from choir, gymnastics, karate, dance, soccer, cheerleading, and band. It will also signify an end to my days of having to chaperone school field trips to the zoo, where I inevitably end up with parrot poop on my head. Another plus? With my kids becoming independent, my car insurance rates will drop. (Sadly, so will my tax deductions. Perhaps the Internal

Revenue Service will start counting male dogs with bathroom hand-icaps as dependents.)

As I revel in these thoughts of freedom, my high schooler has just informed me he's picked the college he'd like to attend—and it's only ten minutes from our home. Looks like my empty-nester plans will have to be put on hold a little bit longer. But I can still dream, can't I?

Livin' Large in Zumba Land

I LIKE TO EAT. A lot. I don't even need a holiday as an excuse to strap on the ol' feed bag. The Vikings have nothing on me when it comes to feasting. My love for food spirals out of control once I lose that first little bit of will power.

My wake-up call came during my annual physical, when I complained to the doctor about my achy back and weak knees. She noticed my recent weight gain and suggested that I lose a few pounds. I wasn't happy about it, but I knew she was right—if I didn't cut back on the chow and start exercising regularly, I'd wind up with a butt the size of Texas.

The first thing I did was join an all-female gym, and I quickly realized that my workout clothes from the Richard Simmons era were sadly outdated. I needed a new gym wardrobe, but visiting a sporting-goods store for clothes to sweat in was an intimidating prospect. I needed a support system.

I made the mistake of inviting my husband along to help me choose my new gear. He was a little TOO enthusiastic at the prospect of his wife getting back into shape. I ditched him in the men's department and went roaming the aisles until I found the women's workout clothes section—and stopped dead in my tracks. Who were these manufacturers kidding? The "large" tops were the size of small sausage casings. I would have been lucky to fit an entire shirt over one arm. Further down the aisle, I came across a row of "grande" tank tops. In white. I envisioned myself sweating through the fabric to the point of transparency and I shuddered.

Then the unthinkable happened—every woman's worst nightmare. My clueless husband held up an armload of colorful men's T-shirts and shouted from across the store, "Hey, Hon, you need a larger size? I found a 2X in the men's department that might fit you!" I knew I should have slapped a muzzle on that man years ago.

After scanning the racks for the largest sizes available, I grabbed a few pairs of yoga pants and some T-shirts with motivational sayings on them such as "Just Do It" and "Live Strong." At that point, the only T-shirt that I was fit to wear was one saying "I Lick Cake Batter Off of Electric Beaters," but apparently they were sold out of those.

I decided it wouldn't be fair to suffer alone in my quest to get back into shape, so I convinced one of my daughters to join the gym with me. Misery loves company, after all. The day we were scheduled to start, I grabbed some Spanx to wear under my shorts. Squeezing my hips into those suckers was like packing seven pounds of cellulite into a three-pound bag. When my daughter and I arrived at the gym, the Spanx were constricting my stomach so tightly I could almost hear them protesting loudly in a Scottish accent: "I can't do it, Captain! I don't have the power!"

We spent our first few torturous days with a personal trainer who taught us how to use the equipment. The entire time my daughter and I were lifting weights, we were also trying not to grimace or sweat like two sumo wrestlers in a sauna. By the time we hit the treadmills that were set at warp speed, I was already perspiring heavily and thinking, "Beam me up, Scotty!" Preferably to a planet that believes chocolate should be the largest block in the food pyramid.

As I struggled to keep up my pace on the evil treadmill, the uncomfortable tightness of the Spanx was becoming further aggravated by my profuse sweating. The dampness was causing my thighs to chafe, and I started to get worried that I might need a large fire extinguisher just to put out the flames. Was healthy living supposed to be this painful?

I decided to try something that was a little less strenuous and a lot more fun, and Zumba class was the answer. I loved the idea of incorporating salsa moves into my exercise routine, because it would trick my brain into thinking it was 1978. The only things that were missing were a spinning disco ball and John Travolta wearing a white leisure suit.

The day of our first Zumba class, I surveyed the group of ladies and was pleased to see a nice mix of ages and body types. Women's shapes are often compared to certain fruits: apples, pears, oranges, and the occasional grapefruit. I was in the midst of a fruit salad, ready to learn some sexy dance moves.

Music with a heavy Latin beat reverberated against the walls and we started hopping around on the wooden floor like Mexican jumping beans. I tried to concentrate on the dance steps, but my mind kept wandering—clearly a defense mechanism against the extreme pain I was in from my previous workouts with the trainer. Rather than listening to the Zumba instructor, I found myself being swept along with the cluttered debris of distracted thoughts:

"Drop it, drop it low girl. Drop it like it's hot. Oh yeah, I got this booty-shakin' thing down … wait. Why isn't my butt moving like everyone else's? And what's that popping sound in my lower back?"

"At least I'm rockin' these new, neon green Nikes. Actually, they kinda look like twin sand barges in the ocean."

"Uh-oh, my junk is jiggling in all the wrong places. I swear I can still see those birthday cupcakes sitting on my hips, mocking me. Damn, these Spanx are still too tight. I wonder what happened to the old Lycra shorts I used to have that sucked in my gut. Who stole my spandex?"

"Geez, I'm tired. Dear Lord, don't let me drop dead in Zumba class! It would scar my daughter for life. Hey, where did she learn to shake her butt like that, anyway? Probably snuck out of her bedroom window to hit the dance clubs on all those nights I thought she was snug in bed."

"Um … am I in Pole Dancing 101 right now? I would have never guessed this many women would be comfortable in booty shorts, playing beaver peek-a-boo! And whose bright idea was it to place mirrors around this brightly lit room? I'm so pale I look like I've been cohabiting with a family of moles."

"HOLY MOTHER OF GOD! Is that what I think it is ... camel toe? I need new pants!"

"Wait ... what fresh hell is this ... more squats? Yoo-hoo, teacher! I'm dying over here. I'm not gonna Busta Rhymes ... I'm gonna busta femur."

"Oh, great! Now I'm sweating so much my makeup is running down my face. I look like I belong at a KISS concert. Huh? Cool down time already? You mean we're done? I made it! I didn't die on the Zumba floor!"

I survived my first class, but all of that salsa music had made me hungry for Mexican food and margaritas. So what did I do? Headed for the nearest taco stand to make my Viking ancestors proud—one double-stuffed enchilada at a time.

Six Good Things About Raising Teenage Girls

AS THE MOTHER of two daughters born only two years apart, I've witnessed my share of teenage drama. Bringing up boys will make your hair turn gray, but bringing up daughters will make it all fall out.

The art of raising girls requires a few essentials which I fondly refer to as "The Three *S's*": Sensitivity, Security, and Shotgun Shells. I'm not going to beat around the bush—a mother has to make certain sacrifices during this time period. I'm thinking, for example, of the times I've had to cross my legs and feel my bladder fill up almost to the point of explosion, just so my daughter and her besties could hole up in the bathroom and take duck-faced Instagram selfies. I'm also thinking of the times I've had to take advantage of the latest sale on aspirin after listening to Bieber beats all day (not to mention One Direction—who, ironically enough, make me want to run in the opposite direction).

For those of you with prepubescent daughters, I've put together this list of six things you can look forward to as your little girls greet their teen years:

1. You'll save money by buying feminine hygiene products in bulk every twenty-eight days. Mothers and daughters often end up with synchronized monthly cycles. This also gives the father a free pass on alcohol consumption and spontaneous man cave time—believe

me, he'll need it after dealing with a bathroom trash can that resembles a hog-slaughtering plant or the fallout of Custer's Last Stand.

2. You will have a team of fashion consultants at your disposal around the clock. Your teenage daughters will pull no punches when convincing you to ditch that sky-blue eye shadow you've been wearing since the eighth grade and the *eau de mothball* perfume that Grandma gave you last Christmas. They will also trick you into spending your entire tax return on a new wardrobe that you will never actually get the chance to wear because they'll "borrow" every last bit of it, right down to your favorite pair of Jimmy Choos.

3. Forget spending extra money on those cable channels that feature reality television programming. You'll be able to enjoy your own live-action drama, with all of the cattiness of *The Bachelor* and all of the trashiness of *Toddlers and Tiaras*, appearing nightly in your living room! Just pour yourself a glass of wine, sit back, and enjoy the show.

4. Teenage daughters will teach you how to twerk and drop it low with women half your age. You'll discover muscles you never knew existed. (Just keep a bottle of ibuprofen on the nightstand if you expect to get out of bed in the morning.)

5. Gun rights activist or not, you'll learn to lock and load when the first boy comes calling.

6. As a child, your daughter will clomp around the house in your high-heeled shoes and pretend to be you. As an adult, she'll fill those shoes and become the woman you're proud to call your best friend.

Closing words of advice: Hide the Jimmy Choos and save the sky-blue eye shadow for your granddaughters. You never know when shoulder pads and parachute pants might come back into fashion.

Nit Picker

WHENEVER I HEAR the words "head" and "lice" strung together in a sentence, I instinctively scratch my scalp. My family experience with these infectious parasites has left me permanently scarred on every imaginable level. The term "nitpicking" took on a whole new meaning the day my oldest daughter began vigorously scratching her head. Oh sure, the elementary school had sent home flyers warning parents about an outbreak of head lice, but my husband and I had remained in complete and utter denial. Not OUR children. Not our CLEAN children.

The invasion happened one day while I was standing outside chatting with a close friend who had dropped by for a visit. My daughter ran out into the sunshine to hug her, and there was a moment of hesitation as my friend stared down at my little girl's scalp. She stood back a moment with an odd expression on her face.

"Do you see what I see?" she asked.

"No, what am I supposed to see?"

My friend parted my daughter's hair, and there, along the highway of her scalp, was a bustling population of tiny, black critters the size of fleas, all of them zipping up and down her shiny, clean hair shafts.

My first reaction was complete and total denial. She had fleas, right? Damn that dog! But when I saw all the little, whitish bubbles stuck to the strands of her hair, I knew EXACTLY what they were.

So began our six-hour introduction to the drama of head lice.

First, there's the embarrassing act of buying the lice shampoo at the drugstore. People tend to give you a wide berth when they see you carrying a nit kit down the aisle. Then comes the delousing of the house, where anything and everything has to be treated like toxic waste. This process entails using a special lice spray on all of the carpets and couches; vacuuming every inch of the floor; washing all of the bedding, towels, and pillows; boiling combs and brushes; steam-cleaning the car; and running all seventy-five Beanie Babies through the dryer at the hottest possible temperature setting.

Working as a team, my husband chose to delouse the house while I examined every strand of hair on my children's heads with magnifying glasses and a nit comb. Six hours and five hundred and thirty-one lice and nits later (yes, I counted), we were parasite free and exhausted. Our house resembled a linen war zone, but I slept better knowing I had killed every one of those suckers—and their little nits, too.

Everything returned to normal and for ten days we lived in ignorant bliss.

Then our daughter began scratching again. "Mommy, they're baaack!"

Denial turned into outrage. Where had the new lice come from? Were some negligent parents out there letting their lice-infested kids roam free? Or perhaps they didn't stay up until 1:00 a.m. pulling every single nit out of their children's hair, like good parents would? They must have cut corners *somewhere* along the line—perhaps they missed a Beanie Baby under the bed—and *we* were the ones who had to pay the price for their negligence.

After the initial denial and outrage came embarrassment. Oh God, the neighbors. There had been sleepovers, carpooling, dinner parties—and we hadn't told a soul, out of fear of being treated like lepers. I accepted that I needed to fess up and warn them, but a neighborhood confessional was going to have to wait. My first call was to the pediatrician to get a prescription shampoo with potentially dangerous side effects—which I merely glanced at with a shrug before squirting the toxic goop onto my children's hair and starting to scrub. The lice literally ran for their lives, running across scalps and foreheads and dropping onto our T-shirts like pirates abandoning ship. I held back screams of dismay and disgust as I once again plucked each parasite from my children's hair and dropped it into a bowl of vinegar.

For weeks we examined each other's hair like monkeys grooming one another in the zoo. We became the resident lice experts—whenever there was an outbreak in the neighborhood, we would strap on gloves and shower caps before examining the child in question. When lice were discovered, the family would go into hibernation for a week until their home and their children were lice-free.

Once or twice that year, when I became lax with my lice prevention duties, the critters managed to find a way to breach security and merrily hop right back onto my children's heads. By that point, gone was the shock, denial, and rage. I would simply switch gears and battle the parasites like any experienced strategist would—with toxic shampoo in one hand and an electric nit zapper in the other.

Eventually we won the war, but don't be surprised if today you still find me with a nit comb in my back pocket. It's always best to be prepared.

Not in My Back Yard

I LOVE MY NEIGHBORHOOD. The majority of families on my street are friendly and helpful. We've been through hurricanes together, survived marital squabbles, conquered a flu epidemic, and dealt with a bout of head lice that kept everyone quarantined and scratching their heads for months.

There is a cozy feeling of unity among us, and I'm fortunate to live in such a peaceful community. But it wasn't always this way. I once lived next to psycho neighbors who snipped our Christmas lights, poisoned our plants, and filmed us whenever we ventured outside. The day those whackadoodles moved was the day I did a little happy dance in the yard as their U-Haul pulled away from the curb.

They say fences make good neighbors. This is especially true if you're dealing with any of these characters on your block:

The Nosy Neighbors. These people spy on the comings and goings of everyone on the street. They know what you ate for dinner, who your favorite drinking buddies are, where your kids spent the night, and how much you spent to sod your yard. A ten-foot fence isn't high enough to keep their nose out of your business.

The Partiers. I love a good party, just not at 3:00 a.m., right outside my bedroom window. Loud karaoke, swimming pools, and cheap booze do not mix.

The Trash Collector. This neighbor's yard is the eyesore of the street. His property is a graveyard for broken-down cars, rust-bucket boats, and dilapidated trailers, all hiding in grass that hasn't seen a mower since the Clinton administration. If you're looking for a used stove or refrigerator, you'll find plenty on his front lawn.

The Noise Maker. Oblivious that some people actually need sleep, this guy starts revving his diesel truck well before the sun comes up, eliminating the neighborhood's need for alarm clocks. He also mows his lawn, trims the hedges, and pressure cleans the house before you've had your first sip of coffee. Somebody needs to slip a Valium into this joker's cup of java.

The Pot Stirrers. These troublemakers have too much time and alcohol on their hands, and they thrive on stirring up trouble. Their goal is to pit neighbor against neighbor and husband against wife by spreading lies and nasty rumors. Obviously they missed their true calling—as scriptwriters for Telemundo soaps.

The Pet Hoarders. Forget stamp collecting. These people collect unneutered dogs and cats, who roam the streets and mate faster than mice in a pet store. These flea-infested pets howl and bark all night, keeping the entire block awake.

If you have neighbors like this, my advice is that you install air gun turrets on your roof and keep watch with night vision goggles and an infrared scope. Welcome to the neighborhood!

Deliver Me from Liver

MANY PEOPLE FROM my generation had parents who thought it was a marvelous idea to feed their children liver. They knew it was high in protein, rich in vitamins, and a good source of iron, so they assumed it was something everyone needed. Which is why, when I was growing up, platters of liver and onions would circulate the dining room table at least once a month. And oh, how I dreaded it.

I would smell it frying in the pan an hour before dinnertime and immediately start contemplating my escape. The nights I had to eat it with onions were bad enough, but when I was forced to eat it with a side of succotash (lima beans mixed with corn), I felt like I was truly experiencing the meaning of hell on Earth. Even a kid can tell that the grouping of those two foods results in an unpalatable combination of flavors, and I would have done anything to get out of eating even one spoonful.

Naturally I would try slipping it to the dog under the table, but Mom always caught onto that ploy, particularly when the dog started gagging—he didn't want to eat that crap any more than I did. My other trick was to fake cough between bites and spit it into my dinner napkin. The problem with that strategy was that my siblings were all doing the same thing, and it didn't take long for my mother to figure out what was in the large, wadded-up napkins she kept finding in the trash.

I was anemic with all of my pregnancies, and the doctors encouraged me to increase my iron intake through various foods and supplements—but I chose spinach and beets to boost my sagging energy levels, because for me, liver was not an option. The liver is the organ that works as the filter system in the body; it produces the nasty, yellowish-green bile that helps with digestion, and it can be full of pesticides and hormones. Who in their right mind would want to eat that? It's gross to look at, it smells weird, and it has the texture of chalk. That's about as appetizing as an offering of blood sausage with cod liver oil on the side.

Today my kitchen is a liver-free zone, even though I'm married to a liver connoisseur. We should have included a liver clause in our wedding vows, exempting me from ever serving the vile meat in our house. But who thinks of these things while in the throes of young love? Thankfully, my husband has found a kindred spirit in our neighbor, who shares his predilection for liver. She fries it up just the way he likes it—smothered in onions. I personally don't care what you smother it with, whether it's ketchup (which allegedly makes everything taste better) or another seasoning—nothing covers up the fact that you're eating organ meat. Just the thought of it makes me want to consider vegetarianism.

After thirty years of marriage, my husband still begs me to cook liver and onions. I tell him to go next door and wolf some down. Then, when he comes home in a liver-induced coma, I thank the Lord for delivering me from liver.

The Ick List

WHEN I WAS YOUNG, I thought one of the most disgusting things in the world was our German shepherd's breath after he'd visited the cat's litter box. Whenever he approached me with white litter sprinkled liberally across his wet nose, I steered clear of any doggie kisses.

Now that I'm a grown woman with children and pets of my own, I've discovered that there are far more disgusting things in life than dogs with litter breath. In fact, in our house alone, there are quite a few things that rate higher on the "Ick Scale"—things that we try desperately to avoid, but which nonetheless invade our everyday lives:

Scary Things in the Refrigerator. Forget green cheese, squishy tomatoes, and furry oranges. My youngest son, who enjoys playing the mad scientist and often leaves his experiments in the refrigerator, can top all of that. On any given day, I might find small bugs encased in the ice cube trays or frozen balls of soiled napkins. And I've learned never to drink anything brown or foamy from the refrigerator—concoctions of that nature often have origins that can be traced to something poisonous from under the kitchen sink.

It's also not unusual for my family members to forget to check the expiration dates on food packages, or to disregard a gallon of milk that has gone sour. It never fails that my husband or one of my children will sample one of these spoiled foods, then with a crinkle of the nose, try to convince me to taste it to see if it's rotten. Why on earth would I want to do that?

Secondhand Towels. Secondhand towels are damp towels that someone else has used and hung back on the rack. After a nice hot shower, there is nothing worse than blindly grabbing one of these towels to dry off my face, only to be assaulted with a cold clamminess and the previous user's scent—usually from an unmentionable area of their anatomy. It's enough to make me want to suds up in the shower all over again.

Cockroaches. In Florida, we have a variety of cockroach known as the palmetto bug, or as I like to refer to it, "the Cadillac of cockroaches." I have a severe cockroach phobia, so for the palmetto bug alone, I keep my exterminator's phone number on speed dial.

The female palmetto bug is especially disturbing. She *flies* in search of a mate, and believe me when I say there's nothing more alarming than a brown-winged torpedo the length of an index finger zinging past my head. What's worse, female palmetto bugs prefer the nighttime, when they can fly freely through the house and roam through the silverware drawer under cover of darkness. If I happen to wake at 3:00 a.m. and switch on a light, I'm rewarded with the sight of cockroaches skittering across my kitchen floor like robbers caught raiding a Wells Fargo truck.

My pulse quickens the minute I spot a pair of long cockroach antennas poking out from a sink or bathtub drain. I scream when I see one skittering across the floor, which only seems to hasten the bug's progress toward my feet. I scream again, and with more urgency, for someone to come kill the invader with a shoe (but not my shoe!). Even then, I won't sleep until the squirming offender is swirling down the toilet bowl.

Things Left Under the Kids' Beds or Behind Their Dressers. I've never understood why it's so difficult for some children to walk three feet to the nearest trash can to dispose of their juice boxes or gum wrappers. And it's worsened with the progression of each of my children. The oldest wouldn't have dreamt of leaving a dirty plate in his bedroom; the youngest wouldn't have dreamt of anything else.

In our fourth child's bedroom, I've found spoons glued to plastic pudding cups and green applesauce cemented to the back side of a drawer. I've uncovered cups full of fermenting orange juice, milk that has long completed its transformation into cottage cheese, and yogurt containers encrusted with dead ants. If I'd saved every breakfast bar wrapper I've ever found under my youngest son's bed, I could have easily wallpapered the Great Wall of China by now.

To be fair, he isn't the only child in this family to be found guilty of using his or her room as a dumpster. My youngest daughter has also been known to leave dozens of half-empty water bottles in every corner of her room (in case of a severe drought?), paper plates stained with pizza grease under her bed, and enough dirty underwear on the floor to strain the confines of our local landfill. I was once so afraid that small rodents had colonized the pile of damp towels and dirty T-shirts in her closet that I could barely bring myself to look inside. It wasn't long before cockroaches laid claim to that end of our house as well.

The Kids' Bathroom. The extra facility down the hall has always been the kids' bathroom. A long time ago, I made the mistake of assuming my children were capable of cleaning their restroom properly, and of doing so on a weekly basis. That proved to be a premature assumption on my part.

I started to notice that the toilet paper roll was rarely changed, offering a disgusting explanation for the discolored tiles at the base of the toilet bowl. I scratched my head in confusion at how my kids' Aquafresh toothpaste could manage to travel the distance between the sink and the shower curtain, leaving a trail of blue globs the size of jellyfish behind. I gaped at their rusty medicine cabinet, the mildewed towels hanging all over every surface, and the shower grout that resembled something growing in a petri dish.

Undoubtedly, the scariest part of their bathroom was always the section behind the toilet. That was No Man's Land—an area the mop couldn't reach and the home of a questionable, stained plunger. Nowadays, the only person brave enough to tackle that region with any consistency is my husband, and you better believe he goes back there with an arsenal of high-grade cleaners. After years of pulling discarded feminine pads off the sides of the garbage can on trash pick-up days, he is no longer intimidated by a few suspicious stains behind the toilet.

Rats. When the time came to remodel certain rooms in our house, there was a unanimous decision to gut the sixty-year-old guest bathroom and transform it into a younger, cleaner model. I couldn't bear to see what was lurking behind those moldy walls, so coward that I was, I took a long morning walk on the day the demolition started. When I returned hours later, the workers were all too happy to show me the little "treasure" they'd found behind the ancient bathtub—a nest of rats.

Rats are the uglier, filthier cousins of my beloved squirrels. We've always enjoyed setting out feeders for the squirrels, but our bathroom construction opened the door for all of their mooching relatives to sneak into my house. While we slept, the rats feasted on breakfast bars, gorged on bagels, and partied with the cocktail peanuts.

Unidentifiable Objects in the Dish Drain. I've never had a garbage disposal in my kitchen sink, which means that the remnants of the day's food wind up trapped in a stainless-steel sink strainer that resembles a miniature colander. The problem is that when the kids wash the dishes, they NEVER clean out the strainer, and it sits for several days collecting the refuse of discarded meals. Spinach is the worst, with meat gristle and miscellaneous fish parts following a close second and third.

Once these things congeal with slippery noodles and slimy chunks of dog food, a certain odor prevails in the kitchen. Since my children would rather donate bone marrow to a distant cousin in Uruguay than clean out that repulsive strainer, that leaves only one person left to handle the task (and that one person isn't going to be me). God bless my husband.

Air Biscuits. This is a polite term for fart clouds. Although most people aren't bothered by their own back-door odors (even after eating refried beans and Brussels sprouts the night before), it's an entirely different olfactory experience when entering into someone

else's gas zone. It happens all the time—while passing fellow jog-
gers on a park trail or circumventing the elderly man looking for
Kaopectate at the grocery store. It's a good indication of how close a
family is when one member can walk into the fart cloud of another
member and clearly identify the offender with one sniff.

The Whole Ball of (Ear) Wax. When my children were little, they
howled and squirmed whenever I would attempt to clean their ears.
Still, they always showed a mix of disgust and fascination with
whatever I extracted. I once made the mistake of comparing their
ear wax to mashed sweet potatoes, and my children spent the next
Thanksgiving warily eyeing the sweet potato casserole and staring
at their grandparents' ears.

Unhappy Feet. As much as I cringe at the sight of unclean ears
and filthy nails, my ick radar goes into overdrive at the sight of dirty
feet—especially if those feet are on my couch or bed. This type of
infraction has always been a particular favorite of our youngest boy.
He has loathed wearing shoes since the very first day I strapped him
into a pair of fancy Stride Rites. When he was still in a car seat, he
would manage to kick off at least one of his shoes on every journey,
causing us to be late to many functions. The rogue shoe would then
disappear into the bowels of the minivan, not to be unearthed until
my son had outgrown it by at least two sizes.

My son spent much of his childhood running gleeful and barefoot through mud puddles and the grassy areas of our yard that
were "reserved for the dog." His aversion to wearing shoes or trim-
ming his toenails carried on well into the middle school years, when
he took great pride in displaying to his friends the longest pinky
toenail known to mankind. Never a girl to mince words, his sister
once took a look at his toes and dubbed them "hobbit feet."

I'm hoping that sooner or later my son will come to his senses
and realize that "hobbit feet" are only acceptable within the *Lord of
the Rings* universe, and that long toenails are useless when one has
no immediate plans to hang upside down with bats.

The Little Stuff. There are so many other small things in life
that cause my stomach to lurch—stepping barefoot into some

unidentifiable, gooey mass on the kitchen floor in the middle of the night; children using fingers instead of tissues on their crusty nostrils (then finding sadistic joy in rubbing the dislodged boogers on their siblings' legs); and gobs of bubble gum stuck to the undersides of coffee tables.

I'm sure I could think of a dozen more things that register on the "Ick Scale," but right now there's an odd scratching sound coming from my bathroom wall, a strange odor emanating from the kitchen sink, and I'm pretty sure I just saw something brown scurrying across the bathroom floor.

Teeth on Edge

MY TEETH BELONG in the Smithsonian, somewhere alongside the display for Prehistoric Cro-Magnon Man. It's my fault—I lived for years on a steady diet of Sugar Babies, Mars Bars, and Twinkies, until a dentist took one look in my mouth and found decay in every tooth in my head. I had so much silver and gold installed that I could have melted it down and opened a pawn shop, but eventually I learned to take good care of my teeth.

Unfortunately, once I hit the premenopausal stage, things began to happen in my mouth. Bad things. Old fillings began washing away, only to be replaced by root canals and crowns.

Several months ago, I heard the dreaded news that no one with a twenty-thousand-dollar mouth wants to hear—I needed to see a periodontist. Impossible! Only old people with walkers go to periodontists, and my teeth look great! What do you mean there's bone loss? Memory loss, yes. Hair loss, sure. But bone loss? How could that possibly have happened? I brush, I Waterpik, and, for God's sake, I carry a huge roll of dental floss in my purse. Could it possibly have something to do with too many years of drinking inferior white wines?

For months I put off going to the periodontist, especially after hearing a detailed description of the gum surgery I would have to endure. Gum flaps? Bone grafts? Sutures? No, double no, and *hell* no.

I was especially hesitant when I learned that the replacement bone would come from cadavers. Or cows. The doctor also mentioned something about coral, but I was still trying to digest the word "cadaver." When the office asked if I was ready to schedule the procedure, it was definitely a "Don't call me, I'll call you" situation.

Time went by and my bone loss increased, ever so slowly. I prayed that my meticulous dental regimen would cure the problem on its own, but no such luck. I even contemplated taking things into my own hands with a pair of pliers and a bottle of tequila, but then I thought of my older son, who'd just had four wisdom teeth pulled. If he could survive oral surgery, then so could I. With the help of a few Valium, of course.

On the day of the appointment, I looked longingly at a crunchy apple, a crusty baguette, and a bag of chewy caramels. It would be weeks, maybe months, before I could indulge in anything like that again. In the doctor's waiting room, my gaze automatically drifted toward the periodontal disease pamphlets. I had to turn away or be sick.

While I was sitting in the dental chair, the Valium kicked in, and within moments I no longer cared if my tooth was being pulled or if an entire cadaver was being jammed into my jaw bone. I just closed my eyes and waited for the last suture to be threaded through my gum. The best part was hearing the doctor advise my husband to pamper me all day and let me sleep for hours on end. For once, I was given permission to be a sloth and watch tacky TV shows from my bed. I was even allowed to hold the coveted remote control.

Later that evening, my husband turned to me and asked, "So which is it? Cow or seventy-nine-year-old man?"

"I'm not sure," I answered, "but if I start mooing or digging through the nightstand drawer for a tube of Polygrip, you'll have your answer!"

Flying Over the Cuckoo's Nest

SOMETIMES I HAVE MOMENTS when I think I'm losing my mind. There used to be a time when I was a compulsive organizer and proud of it. The books on my shelf were stored according to size and genre. All of my photo albums were neatly labeled and shelved in chronological order. My closet was color-coordinated, as were the contents of my underwear drawer, and my shoes fit snugly in shoe trees organized by heel length and seasonal use. Freakish to some, but a necessity for me to keep my sanity in check.

Back then, I was never late for a function, and I could effortlessly juggle work with the kids' extracurricular activities, all while entertaining company and serving up a homemade five-course meal, like Martha Stewart. Wonder Woman had nothing on me.

Everything changed when I hit menopause.

It started with the car keys. It took me thirty minutes one morning to find them, and it was no wonder, because they were hanging out in the refrigerator next to the yogurt. I swore I didn't leave them in there—surely someone was playing a prank on me.

My glasses disappeared the following week, which left me half-blind, bumping into furniture, and eating what I thought was a brownie, but turned out later to be a charcoal briquette. Please explain to me how you're supposed to find missing glasses when you need your glasses to find them!

It wasn't long before I was forgetting my appointments at the salon (which resulted in hair that looked and felt like a worn-out Brillo pad) and mixing up my appointments just about everywhere else. The last time I showed up at the dentist's office to get a cavity filled, the nurse reminded me I was there for a colonoscopy. Oh yes, they were going to fill a cavity all right.

What the hell was happening to me? Did all the crazy, drunken weekends from my college years really destroy THAT many brain cells? (I knew that weekend in St. Louis with my sorority sisters was a mistake.) Was this some kind of karmic punishment for all those times I poked fun at my husband for being absentminded and easily distracted? Well, now the tables had turned, and somewhere between this birthday and the last, my mind had taken a seat on the crazy train right next to his.

Distraction is never a good thing, but it's especially treacherous in the kitchen, like when I add salt instead of sugar to a recipe, or bake ~~a loaf of bread~~ a lumpy pancake that even the dog turns away from: "Lady, I may be just a dog, but even I have some standards." And when the dog is insulted, he pees on the furniture to exact his revenge—or maybe he does it because I keep forgetting to walk him.

Some days I forget to take my vitamins or eat plenty of whole grains. This can be dangerous for all the wrong reasons—something akin to a septic tank on the brink of failure. Other times, I forget things that are less important, like whether or not I put detergent in the washing machine, or where I put the remote control (under my butt). My mother suggested that I start doing crossword puzzles to sharpen my mind. I tried it, but I think my brain is already too far gone because I couldn't remember the three-letter word for donkey.

While it has been a relief to learn that memory loss associated with menopause is normal—think of the two as holding hands and skipping gleefully down a path toward their best friend dementia—it's fairly disturbing to discover the alarming rate at which it's happening. I can't help but think of all the menopausal women out there who, as we speak, are forgetting to clean the house, cook dinner, or pick up the kids after school. And they aren't even the worst-case examples. I feel for those of us who are *really* in the throes of memory loss—taking the wrong exit ramps to work and ending up at nail salons and bingo halls in downtown Miami.

So what am I going to do? Make myself a margarita (or three) to help myself forget what I can't remember. By the way, have you seen my glasses? Or the remote control?

One Zit at a Time

WHAT'S UP WITH menopausal acne? I don't eat mountains of chocolate or greasy food. I don't use oily anti-aging products, and I certainly don't harbor any kind of sexual frustration. So why is it that every couple of months I get a cluster of red bumps on my face? Is it in preparation for a phantom period? There is no more period, so there should be no more blemishes—at least that's the way *I* see it. Yet there they are, like red, blistery groundhogs, popping up overnight as if to predict another six weeks of winter.

I never had much acne as a teenager, so maybe this is payback time. (Although I do remember attending some sort of college sorority dance looking like Rudolph the Red Nose Reindeer. No amount of foundation or powder in the world could cover up *that* Bozo the Clown nose.)

Conventional wisdom teaches us that pimples are often stress-induced, but in my case, they seem to crop up whenever I'm at my happiest—like ten minutes before I'm about to meet with someone I haven't seen in ten years, when I'm preparing for a romantic evening with my husband, or when I'm getting ready to pose for the annual family holiday photo.

"Geez, what the heck is that thing on Marcia's forehead? It looks like a third eye!"

"The tip of Aunt Marcia's nose sure is red ... is she the one who likes her wine?"

"Mommy! Look at Nonni's humongous boil!"

Why do we experience this second wave of blemishes later in life? Isn't it enough that we suffer through acne during our years of teenage angst? It just doesn't seem fair. I no longer get a period, but I still go through all of the symptoms of one: bloating, raging, and crying over anything remotely sentimental. It makes me want to eat chips, slam a door in someone's face, and feed a child in Guyana.

It brings me to this question: Why haven't they invented menopausal pimple prevention cream? Probably because there would be too many side effects: permanent rosacea, cankles, increased cellulite, and a third spare tire around the middle. Or an inflamed gobbler, bat wing fat, a unibrow, and a sixth toe on the left foot.

I've tried a whole host of different solutions—from expensive dermabrasion to chemical peels that leave my face looking like a freshly steamed lobster. (I've heard that some women go so far as to rub cat litter and cream on their faces for a smooth complexion.) I cleanse and moisturize and I have to say that most days my skin looks pretty darn good. But then there are those mornings that I wake up with one singular pimple that somehow evolves into a riotous cluster of acne by the end of the evening.

At this rate, I'm afraid I'll be ordering Proactiv from my granny chair at the old folks' home, along with my usual case of Metamucil. You know what? That kitty litter face scrub isn't sounding all that bad.

Adventures in Blogging

I'VE ALWAYS BEEN technologically challenged. I was the last one in the family to learn how to use a DVD player, operate a cell phone, and turn on a computer. Several years ago, my husband decided to slowly ease me into the world of technology ownership by purchasing a hot pink iPod for my birthday. After dozens of failed attempts to find and store my favorite songs (I couldn't figure out how to scroll through playlists or adjust the volume), I threw the expensive gadget at my husband and told him to take the stupid thing back to the store for a refund.

A glutton for punishment, the poor man tried once again, and gave me a Kindle the following Christmas—this time making sure to inch away slowly as I unwrapped the present. I plastered a smile on my face, thanked him for the lovely gift, and promptly deposited it in my underwear drawer, with no intention of ever using it. I liked my paperback novels, and no fancy gadget could ever replace them.

A year later, my kids found the Kindle, dusted it off, and shoved it into my hands. It was time for me to step out of the disco era, they said, and learn something about today's technology. I relented. It took a while, but I finally got the hang of it and actually began looking forward to reading my favorite novels on the Kindle at bedtime.

Receiving a new laptop the following Christmas forced me to enroll in a computer class aimed at the geriatric set. I soon realized that learning my way around the Kindle had been like dipping a mere toe into the pool of technological advances. A laptop, however, was like diving in head first.

For months, I tinkered around on the computer and discovered how much I liked emailing back and forth with friends who had given up on such ancient relics as stationery, ink pens, and postage stamps. I forged on and slowly grasped the exhilarating freedom of Internet exploration. I had stepped into an amazing new world, and there was no way I could ever crawl back into the dark cave from whence I'd come, where finger-painting with berry juice on stone walls was the norm. Google became my favorite word of the day, and I wanted everyone to know that I was finally hip to using a computer.

Then I discovered blogging. Within days, I joined what felt like a secret society known as the blogosphere, and I was hooked. I read hundreds of blogs, contacted authors, and eventually set up my own blog site. I was fascinated and intimidated by the concept of exploiting my life on the Internet—an unpredictable place where I could be either loved or ridiculed for my point of view. But I figured, what the heck? What did I have to lose other than my dignity? That ship had sailed a long time ago.

With a glass of chardonnay in one hand and my laptop in the other, I composed my first blog post. I'll admit it was much easier to write after the third glass of vino.

Jumping into the blogosphere was one of the best decisions I've made, but it was not without some sacrifices. My addiction to blogging immediately caused setbacks in several areas of my Donna Reed lifestyle—changes my family did not embrace. Household chores took a backseat to my writing. I seldom had time to run the vacuum cleaner—you could have knitted a sweater and matching scarf with the amount of dog hair embedded in our carpets. My family figured out that I hadn't done laundry in months. I was only able to get away with spritzing their dirty clothes with Febreze for so long.

Much to everyone's dismay, the microwave became my best friend. Since I no longer had time to cook, I learned to be creative when it came to putting dinner together. Each night I would present a surprise smorgasbord of leftovers from the dark depths of my freezer. It was amazing what I could create with a lone hot dog, a sad-looking waffle, and a bag of freezer-burned peas.

To help fuel my nonstop thirst for word artistry, I developed a raging caffeine addiction. Forget a single pot of coffee—I wanted the whole damn bag. On one particular day, when I had trouble keeping my eyes open, I considered chewing on coffee grounds for breakfast. This concerned my husband, who was convinced that caffeine overload was turning me into a whirling dervish akin to the Tasmanian Devil.

Lack of sleep became another issue I had to deal with as an obsessed writer. Thanks to a hyperactive muse and regular bouts of insomnia, I morphed into a nocturnal creature, related to the animals who think clearest at night. The sleeplessness caused dark, angry circles around my eyes, like those on a raccoon.

Even when I was able to snatch a few hours of precious sleep, my nightmares turned into blogmares. I was plagued by odd dreams that involved Teletubbies, giant spiders, and Spanish-speaking goats. I'm not sure if it was the abundance of caffeine that caused these colorful dreams, or if my creative juices were just on overdrive, but either way, Freud would have had a field day with my brain.

My frustrated husband eventually grew weary of my blogging addiction and complained that he rarely saw his wife. He wondered if I'd gone underground, or entered the witness protection program—the untouched stash of Butterfinger bars in the candy dish was evidence that I'd been missing for a long time. The kids often stood beside my desk and waited for me to acknowledge them, but my brain was usually blogger mush. When I would finally look up from my computer screen, I would stare at them and ask:

"Who are you people?"

"We're your children!"

"I have kids? When did that happen?"

My husband tried a different tactic to grab my attention. "Honey, there's a herd of elephants stampeding down the street, and they're headed for our house!"

"That's okay, Babe. Just sprinkle mozzarella cheese on them, and bake them at four hundred degrees."

My family tried plying me away from the computer with wine, chocolate truffles, a Disney vacation, and a puppy, but it was no use. I was lost in a blogger daze.

And then the unthinkable happened. Our Internet went down during a storm, and I was without my beloved computer for an entire weekend. At first, panic set in. Then came anger and blame, similar to the Kübler-Ross model of the five stages of grief. I wandered aimlessly through the house and checked the cable connection every five minutes to see if the power had been restored.

Concerned by the glazed look in my eyes, my family began searching for a Bloggers Anonymous support group.

Without the Internet to suck up hours of my time, I was forced to brush the thick layer of dust off the stove and actually use the appliance to cook healthy meals for my family. I also tackled the overflowing baskets of laundry. Some of the pants were so dirty, they could have walked themselves over to the laundry machine and jumped right in.

After wiping the film from my eyes, I began to see my family clearly for the first time in months. "Oh yeah, now I recognize you! You're the son I gave birth to nineteen years ago. And there's the daughter I just celebrated a twenty-first birthday with! Hey, isn't that handsome man over there with a beer in one hand and the television remote in the other, my husband?"

My family was more than happy to welcome me back to the land of the living.

The Internet was finally restored a few days later and my computer hummed back to life. I circled it a few times, caressed its shiny top, and dreamed of all the new blog posts I wanted to write. I knew there were hundreds of emails just waiting to be opened, but I resisted the urge to touch the keys and focused on my family instead.

The blogging obsession is still here today. I've just learned to harness that energy into more productive things, like organizing my three hundred bottles of nail polish or cleaning out the dryer lint trap. But some nights, when the house is quiet and the caffeine is singing through my veins, I can't resist opening my laptop and blogging with the rest of the insomniacs of the world—as long as my husband isn't waiting outside with the garden shears, ready to snip the cable line.

Save the Drama for Your Mama

ONCE UPON A TIME, I was a very tolerant person. But somewhere between screaming my head off in the delivery room and the onset of my first hot flash, I became *a lot less* tolerant. It didn't occur all at once, instead happening gradually, like the changing of the leaves at the onset of autumn. Like them, I went from vibrant green to crusty brown.

In my youth, I never understood the impatience and general crankiness of elderly people. Now that I'm a mid-lifer, I feel like I have a license to be cantankerous. It doesn't take much to spark my temper, or for someone to tap dance all over my last sane nerve.

For example, it never used to bother me when people would run out and buy the newest gadget on the market (back in the old days, we're talking things like microwaves, cordless phones, and miniature cassette-tape players.) But now, it chaps my hide to no end that everyone HAS to own the latest technological wonder: the iPhone, the iPad, the iBidet, and the iDon'tCare.

I've also become increasingly annoyed by people who feel compelled to give me constant updates on their latest exercise regimen and/or diet plan. I'll be standing in line at the bakery and someone behind me will say, "I really shouldn't—after all, I just lost five pounds!" Meanwhile I'm thinking, "Butter cream or chocolate mocha frosting on those cupcakes?"

I don't have time for people with Type A personalities anymore. When I was younger, I was often accused of being one myself, and I felt flattered by the accusations. I admired those powerful, aggressive people fighting for a cause. Now their passion exhausts me. I don't have patience for their soapbox drama.

I'm also losing my patience for people who brag. When I'm feeling particularly grumpy, the last thing I want to hear is how great your expensive European vacation was, how awesome your kid is at underwater basket-weaving, and how excited you are about that lucky lottery ticket you bought. Unless you're feeling charitable enough to pay off my mortgage, I really don't want to know how the planets keep aligning perfectly for you while I'm stuck in the crossfire of a meteor shower.

What disturbs me more than anything is menopausal fatigue. I used to have the energy of a toddler. I could simultaneously flip a pancake, nurse a baby, donate one hundred dollars to the Penguin Tuxedo Fund, and practice my Irish dancing steps. Now I'm yawning at 10:30 a.m. (after two cups of coffee strong enough to invigorate the dead). All I want to do is hibernate in bed until somebody rings the dinner bell. "I WAKE FOR STEAK!"

And what's up with the fickle bladder in middle age? I used to be like a camel, storing fluids for days. Now this camel needs a urostomy bag.

I may have hit my fifties like the last person stuck in the corner of a bounce house, with no one there to pull me out—but never fear, this middle-aged mama will persevere.

Facebook Follies

WHEN FACEBOOK FIRST became popular, my kids set up an account for me, but I rarely looked at it. In fact, I thought the notion of spending all that time chatting with people I hadn't seen since I carried a Howdy Doody lunchbox to school was kind of silly. I was also sharing the old, clunky family computer with three other people in the house, so it seemed pointless to try and get into a juicy online conversation with an old friend while my kids were hovering nearby, waiting for their turns to neglect homework in favor of socializing on Facebook.

Life changed the day my husband surprised me with my very own computer. It was the Holy Grail of communication for me, and every time I lifted the lid on my laptop, I swore I could hear the "Hallelujah Chorus." Suddenly, I couldn't get enough of being online—I was zipping through videos, news, and emails, all while googling stupid stuff like "kangaroos trained to play Ping-Pong in Australia." It was a heady experience, all that power at my fingertips. With one click, I had access to THE SECRETS OF THE UNIVERSE, or at least great recipes for low-fat meatloaf.

So I decided to give Facebook another chance. I soon discovered a whole community filled with hundreds of people who, at one time or another, had been important in my life. I badgered my kids daily to help me improve my profile, upload nice (flattering) pictures, and locate every human being I've ever known since the day I exited my mother's womb. "Hey, remember me? We shared a mat together during nap time in Mr. Jim's kindergarten class."

My kids are now nauseated by my Facebook enthusiasm. They never expected this old fossil to become a Facebook aficionado. I'm obsessed with it—not only can I catch up with old friends, I can share recipes, videos, music, and photos of the grandchildren, all while getting good advice on how to stop my dog from pooping on the living room carpet. I can change my status daily or even hourly, and there is always someone out there reading it, ready to send me a smile or lend a sympathetic ear to my daily grumblings.

Unfortunately, my new addiction began to disrupt my family life and affect my health. I started to suffer from NBS (Numb Butt Syndrome), a direct consequence of sitting in a chair for hours while browsing Facebook. Keeping a spotless home and spending three hours perfecting my mother's lasagna recipe were no longer priorities for me. Dust ball farms sprouted under the beds, and my cobweb-festooned house came to closely resemble Miss Havisham's home in *Great Expectations*. Household chores also dropped low on the priority list, and my poor family was compelled to survive on ramen noodles and cans of green beans that had been sitting in the back of my pantry since 2006.

My family reached a breaking point, staged an intervention, and forced me into counseling for my Internet addiction. After completing a twelve-step program, I was presented with a "Just Say No to Facebook" T-shirt—but sadly, it was all in vain, for I could NEVER give up Facebook. It's my lifeline to an entire community of friends, and I'm not prepared to sacrifice the voyeuristic peek into the world it offers.

Although I love Facebook, it has very few guidelines for users to adhere to. You can get away with just about anything you want to post on your wall. To improve the overall experience for everybody, I think Facebook should design a manual that advises against the following:

Game Requests. There are plenty of addicting games out there, some of which border on the cultish, and I avoid them like the plague. The amount of time I spend on the Internet is already long enough without having to mainline *Candy Crush Saga* or convince someone to buy me a pig for my virtual farm.

Drunk Facebooking. You've heard of drunk texting? Drunk Facebooking is worse. Do NOT get lubed up on cheap ale or boxed wine, stalk old boyfriends and/or girlfriends, and write morose messages on your wall about feeling unloved or underappreciated.

Selfies. I enjoy looking at profile pictures, but after a while the selfies all start to look the same. They're usually taken at a high angle so that the person in the picture looks like they've had a face lift or BOTOX injections. Okay, I'm guilty of selfies like this, but so is most of the female population over the age of forty.

Too Much Information. I don't need to know that the Burrito Supreme you just inhaled at Taco Hell is making you poop like a tri-colored bean piñata.

Political Pundits. During the last election, the candidate bashing on Facebook was unconscionable. Unfortunately, I was forced to muddle through it just to read posts from others like me who prefer not to use the site as a political platform. Is it so hard to keep your political opinions to yourself?

Photo Tagging. REAL friends do not tag you in unflattering pictures. It defeats the purpose of all your selfies. Nothing is worse than schlepping through Lowe's to check out the assortment of sprinkler heads, then logging on to your Facebook feed and discovering that someone out there has tagged you in a picture from last year's holiday office party. You know the one—it's that questionable photo of you riding on the shoulders of a coworker and wearing an alligator snout on your face.

The worst is when your kids post god-awful pictures while you're out of town (and miles from any Wi-Fi hotspots), and you have NO IDEA that the entire universe is seeing the REAL YOU in living color. This can scar you for life, and you'll end up shouting in your sleep, "DELETE! DELETE!"

Family Drama. I don't want to read Act Three of your family argument about the cousin who slept with your sister's boyfriend, and I certainly don't need to hear the blow-by-blow account of your in-law who swears he didn't father your neighbor's new baby. If you want the whole world in on your drama, apply for a guest spot on *The Jerry Springer Show*.

Health Issues. It's not necessary to tell everyone the details of your uncle's testicular problems or your recent bladder infection. And if you're seriously depressed, share it privately with your closest friends or seek professional help, rather than alarm all of the people who follow your status updates. (Unless your goal is for sympathy chocolate. In that case, it just might be worth a large box of Godiva.)

Vacation Pictures. Although I'm happy for friends who are fortunate enough to be able to afford a little rest and relaxation, I'm also a tad bit jealous. While they're sipping wine at an outdoor cafe in the south of France, I'm vacuuming up clots of dog hair and scooping Tootsie Rolls out of the cat's litter box.

So why, if I have all of these complaints, am I still addicted to Facebook? In a nutshell— FRIENDS. We share funny jokes and memes, support one another through the tough times, and celebrate our victories together. I can connect with people I haven't seen since grade school while relaxing in my pajamas with curlers in my hair. It's like one big online reunion, minus the pricey reservations and the stress over what makeup or clothing will best shave ten years off of my appearance. (They have my selfies for that.)

In the meantime, I'll be the disheveled woman behind the computer in a dog hair-covered bathrobe with toast crumbs in her lap.

Pigs, Poodles, and Possums

IF WRITER'S BLOCK didn't stump me so often, I'd have twelve novels written by now, and I'd be using all my royalties to build an adults-only amusement park, complete with a margarita waterfall. But it does plague me here and there, and it's at those moments when I turn into a professional procrastinator.

This is how it starts:

5:45 a.m.: Obnoxious alarm clock jars me awake. I want to yank it from the wall and toss it out the window onto the neighbor's lawn. It wouldn't matter because they get up at the ass crack of dawn to rev up their diesel trucks. On my night stand sits the "To Do" list I scribbled the night before, when there was still adrenaline coursing through my veins after watching a rousing episode of *Judge Judy*. In the bleak morning light, that "To Do" list becomes a "GO TO HELL" list. No way am I getting up this early to make breakfast for everyone; this is why God invented granola bars and oatmeal-on-the-go. I slap the snooze button for fifteen more minutes.

6:00 a.m.: Just as I drift off into Neverland, I hear a nagging buzzer go off and wonder if I'm on a new game show called *Wheel of Misfortune*. I guess I'd better wake up.

6:15 a.m.: Coffee. My morning elixir. Jumper cables to my heart. Now I'm ready to work.

6:30 a.m.: I'm hit with the realization that just because my body is doing the happy dance doesn't mean that my brain has caught onto the steps. Need more coffee.

7:00 a.m.: I'm staring at a blank computer screen, convinced that my muse has purchased a one-way ticket to Bora Bora and is completely content to sip Mai Tais on the shore while I struggle to post something witty on my blog.

7:30 a.m.: Still staring at the same blank computer screen. I take a break to pick dog hair off my T-shirt and make a daisy chain out of paper clips. Then I scroll through Facebook and comment on status updates: "Wow Camille! You sure look wasted in those office party pictures. Do people still do that kind of stuff on copy machines?" "Aw, Cynthia, I just LOVE little Tommy's mullet. Is he channeling Billy Ray Cyrus?"

9:30 a.m.: Instead of staring at the computer screen, I'm now staring out of my home-office window. When did the neighbors get a hairless cat? Oh, that's a possum rummaging around in the trash can. I didn't know possums liked beer.

10:00 a.m.: Glance at Facebook again to see if anyone commented on my latest status update: "Is it too early to add whiskey to my coffee cup? LOL!"

10:30 a.m.: Check refrigerator to see if anyone left an amazing surprise in there for me to eat, like an ice cream bar or leftover pizza.

11:00 a.m.: Back on the computer. I begin typing a blog entry: "Hello Readers! I'm hyped up on caffeine and shaky as hell, but my brain has a log jam and I … oh look! Puppies!"

11:30 a.m.: Gotta get this blog post going. Whoa, what's this? New outdoor decorating ideas on Etsy? Pot-bellied pigs for sale on Craig's List?

1:00 p.m.: I stalk other blog sites for inspiration. They're all good. Damn good. Rather than inspired, I end up feeling insecure and overwhelmed. I pick up the phone and call a friend for moral support.

2:30 p.m.: Damn possum is back. Brought some of his buddies. I didn't know they could carry a six-pack and beach chairs.

4:30 p.m.: Wake up to find the imprint of a computer keyboard on my forehead.

5:00 p.m.: Feed and walk dogs while trying to figure out something clever, yet appetizing, for dinner. My family is slowly but surely catching on to the fact that I'm recycling leftovers, and just tossing in pasta or rice to confuse them.

8:00 p.m.: Back on the computer. Something skitters across the floor and under my desk. Could have been a cockroach. Or that possum. Call husband to exterminate whatever predator is stalking me.

10:00 p.m.: Loud cheering from the TV room. My family is either watching a Dolphins' game or *Keeping Up with the Kardashians*. I need to investigate.

12:00 a.m.: Computer screen still blank. So is my brain. Time to reboot both. The possums are now sitting around a campfire, singing "Kumbaya" and making s'mores.

Surely tomorrow will be a more productive day, as long as a parade of pugnacious pot-bellied pigs and prancing pink poodles doesn't pass by my office window.

The Box

IN MY HALL CLOSET, there is a box hidden beneath bath towels and bed sheets. Inside of it are the scraps of memories of a child I never had the chance to know: a lock of hair, some yellowed snapshots, and the black-and-white ink print of a foot no larger than my thumb. There was a time when I needed to open the box daily to reassure myself that the baby had actually existed, if only for a brief moment in my arms.

I keep the box on a high shelf, crowded between old baby clothes my children have long outgrown, and the tattered, smudged drawings from their early kindergarten days. I seldom think about it, until it's time to reorganize the closet to make room for the clutter of new memories. My hand brushes across the worn flaps and I feel the need to open it again, despite the years that separate me from that part of my past.

The box has been stored in the closet for two decades, yet every time I see it, I am surprised by its presence and what it once meant to me—the hopes and dreams of a young mother carrying twins. I lift the lid slowly and touch the silky wisp of blonde hair inside. Folded neatly underneath the sympathy cards and letters is a small cotton blanket. My hand automatically smooths the satin edge and slowly I bring it to my cheek, remembering the softness of the little boy it once held.

There was a time when I believed the box was all that I had left of Jason, until one morning when I looked into his twin sister's eyes and unexpectedly saw his smile. She'd just taken her first steps around the coffee table and had rewarded me with her toothless grin. I cried then for the miracle of having such a special baby, and for the twin boy that I'd never see take his first steps, play catch with his father, splash in the surf, star in a school play, walk across the stage for his high school diploma, or escort his new bride down a church aisle. Although I missed him and often wondered what it would have been like to raise twins, I realized early on how blessed I was to have his twin sister, who brings me so much joy to this day.

When I was younger, it was very painful to open Jason's box. It forced me to face a loss I never understood. Today, it represents more than that. It reminds me of the courage it took me to work through that loss—something I never could have accomplished without the love of my family and the power of faith. The box was part of my healing process. Every time I sifted through its contents, I became stronger.

I'll never forget Jason or the softness of his skin when I cradled him in my arms. Although our time together was brief, he taught me some valuable lessons. Our children are a blessing, and the special moments we share with them are the little miracles in our lives that make up the memories we carry in our hearts when we grow old.

For J.

Your voice is hidden in the hum
of a respirator, each breath
the weight of a stone
in this sterile room
where shadows of infants
drift across hospital walls
leaves that break loose

from summer trees
scatter into fall

Clouds shift in your eyes
the hard blue of summer
the sorrow of lullabies
you will never know
only my hand against the pale moon
of your face
spirit lifting from my fingers
into the light
your small shadow etched
into the darkening sky.

Life in the Unemployment Lane

A FEW THANKSGIVINGS AGO, when most people were count-
ing their blessings, I was the pessimistic Grinch seeing a glass that
was half empty. The month before, my husband had unexpectedly
lost his job, and our world had been turned upside down. It felt as if
someone had stomped on the brakes while we weren't wearing seat
belts; not only did we lose our income, but our health care as well.

To say that life was a challenge during this time is an under-
statement. A trap door had opened beneath our feet, and while the
rope to climb out was within our grasp, it was very difficult to reach.
My husband, who had been born during the Stone Age, could not
compete with the Generation X applicants clamoring for the same
jobs. He was a Commodore 64 stuck in an iPad world.

My husband's routine changed dramatically during this time in
his life. Instead of spending eight hours at a job, he would spend
eight hours digging under couch cushions and beneath the car's
floorboards, in search of loose change with which to play the lottery.
He couldn't walk past a vending machine without checking the coin
return for stray nickels and dimes.

He began needing a two-hour nap in the middle of each day,
particularly after the mass quantities of cheap food he would consume in order to counteract his boredom. He'd stand at the kitchen
counter and squirt cheese from a can directly into his mouth, then

wash it down with a handful of crackers. Don't judge—it was a quick, simple meal. Gone were the days of a good Porterhouse steak; our dinners had been reduced to Spam and corn out of a can.

To keep himself busy, my husband took on projects. He trimmed all the hedges into Disney topiaries, painted the shed camouflage, and dug up our yard to install a new sprinkler system, which left the grass looking like a groundhog transit system.

There were some positive sides to having my better half at home all day. He tackled the pantry that I had neglected for a lifetime, alphabetizing and color coding all of the soup cans, boxed meals, and cake mixes. He also turned into Mr. Clean—the rain gutters and the tile grout in the shower were immaculate.

Being unemployed meant that we got to sleep in as late as we wanted. We also had time to explore every chapter of the Kama Sutra—until one of us ended up in the chiropractor's office. Eventually my husband found a new job and life returned to normal: sack lunches, regular income, and juicy steaks on the grill.

That Thanksgiving when he was jobless, our turkey may have been the size of a Cornish game hen, but we were still grateful. We were broke, but wealthy in all the ways that counted most.

In Sickness and In Health

FOR AS LONG AS I can remember, my husband has been haunted by the ghosts of old injuries. I may be the Queen of Klutz, but my guy is likewise the King of Injuries Past, and he has visited the emergency room countless times over the course of our marriage. An unfortunate accident on the baseball field while in his teens left him with the knee caps of an eighty-year-old man; they snap, crackle, and pop like a bowl of Rice Krispies cereal whenever he pushes himself off the couch.

It doesn't help that this middle-aged man thinks with the brain of a twenty-five-year-old. He never turns down a challenge on the basketball court, and will gladly snap on a knee brace just to try and keep up with the teenagers. One year, when my son's friends gathered in the front yard to perform stunts with their skateboards and BMX bikes, my husband decided he didn't want to miss out on all the fun. He assured the boys that he had been quite the cyclist in his youth, and that there wasn't a ramp around that he couldn't conquer. Sensing a challenge, the teens goaded my husband into reliving his boyhood days. He swaggered over to the bike with the confidence of Evel Knievel before hopping on and peddling full force down the street. Up he went, over the ramp, gliding through the air with the glory of youth shining in his eyes.

Then his feet slipped off the pedals, and the bike landed with a resounding thud on the hard pavement. It's a good thing we were already past the procreation stage in our lives, because my husband lost the use of his family jewels that day. Time to trade in the BMX bike for a motorized wheelchair.

When my youngest daughter turned eleven, she invited a group of friends over for a slumber party. While the girls ate pizza and watched spooky movies, my husband came up with a brilliant idea that only a prepubescent teenage boy would admire: he donned a rubber monster mask and crept outside to give the girls a little scare.

Just as they were settling down into their sleeping bags, my husband popped up and pounded on the window to frighten them. The girls shrieked, glass shattered, and the "monster" became strangely quiet. That's when I noticed the two red fountains pulsing from his wrists. My husband had inadvertently sliced them both open on the broken windowpane, and was in need of immediate medical attention.

The paramedics found it hard to believe that a middle-aged man would skulk around his own backyard wearing a monster mask. If they'd seen him the week before, in a Velcro suit and climbing up the adhesive wall at Disney's Pleasure Island after too much Jägermeister, they'd understand.

Alcohol has always been the liquid courage that prompts men to do stupid things, and my husband is no different. After one rousing game of beer pong with a group of college students, my overly confident husband challenged his two strapping sons to a wrestling match. Why not? After all, he'd been the captain of the wrestling team in high school—thirty years ago (which explains why he ended up face first in a nightstand drawer, waking up the next morning to a deviated septum and two black eyes).

Since then, there have been countless knee injuries, twisted ankles, sore backs, torn ligaments, broken toes, sprained fingers, and black eyes, and I can't help but wonder if my husband's coworkers have ever speculated on the nature of our marriage. Menopausal women do have tempers, after all.

I Need a What?

COLONOSCOPY. The scary "C" word. It was something I'd been putting off for a while. Unfortunately, once I hit fifty, I couldn't delay it any longer; my husband dragged me kicking and screaming into the doctor's office. Like most people, I was seriously against the idea of a camera being shoved up my you-know-what.

Unfortunately, colonoscopies are a middle-aged reality. There's no running from them or dodging their necessity. Believe me, I tried and failed. What I did manage to do, however, was convince my husband to schedule *his* procedure on the same day as my own: "The family that gets colonoscopies together stays together!"

My husband was four years overdue, so he was anxious to get it done. He has a history of polyps, so he needed the double whammy—two cameras shoved in two orifices for the price of one. In fact, his very first question to the doctor was whether the camera they were going to use to explore his colon was going to be the same one they put down his throat. The grinning doctor assured him that, yes, it was indeed the same camera, but not to worry. They would explore the throat first before heading south. That's when I interrupted the conversation: "You're not using the same camera on me! I don't want the leftovers—schedule me first!"

After much ribbing from our friends and a lot of great advice ("Use Gatorade to mix the powdered medicine;" "Use wet wipes for your behind, because, trust me, you'll need them"), we faced the daunting task of getting through the "day of preparation." The entire day before our procedures, we could drink only clear liquids. No solid foods were allowed. We also had to swallow a nasty, powdered medicine, dissolved in liquid and drunk by the gallon, in order to clear out our colons. Our butts were about to take us on a wild ride at the speed of light.

On the prep day, I felt like a contestant on *Survivor*. Twenty-four hours of no food? To a food junkie like me, that was the equivalent of serving twenty-four *years* in jail. I was chugging chicken broth and apple juice until I felt like I was going to start clucking and pecking at fruit. I was dying of starvation, ready to forage in the flower beds or gnaw on the wooden sofa legs.

My husband was just as miserable. I've never seen him look so longingly at a handful of pretzels as he did that day when our son started munching on some. We agreed that even the dogs were starting to look pretty tasty. The doctor had instructed, "Only clear liquids." I idly wondered if that included gin and vodka.

At 2:00 that afternoon we were due to start drinking the "special cleansing fluid," or as I later came to think of it, "the stuff that makes you poop uncontrollably." We mixed the powdered prescription medicine with lemon-lime Gatorade, and began chugging. It was like the drinking games we played in college—my husband and I stood side by side at the sink and tried to out-chug one another. I could almost hear the frat boys chanting, "Go, go, go!"

So far, so good.

Fifteen minutes later, as we were sitting on the sofa and watching The Food Network (we were gluttons for punishment), I heard the first rumbling. It sounded like Mount Vesuvius getting ready to explode. I turned to my husband and asked: "Was that your stomach or mine?" His stomach replied, "Gurgle, gurgle." Then we both screamed, "OH MY GAWD!" and the race to the bathroom began.

Thank goodness we have two toilets in our house because if we hadn't, someone would have been sticking their fanny in a bucket. These were not bowel "urges" by any stretch of the imagination—these were bowel *demands*. Too bad I didn't have a television in my bathroom, because I sure could have used one after sitting in there for five hours doing colon gymnastics.

The day of the procedure, I was so hyper-focused on what I was going to eat once I woke up from the anesthesia that I no longer feared what was going to be done to me. I wondered if they'd serve me steak and a big baked potato in the recovery room. That would be a nice thing to wake up to after being molested by a small camera.

As promised, I was wheeled into the surgical room before my husband. I waved a feeble "goodbye" to him as I rolled past, and he gave me the thumbs-up. It was a bit disconcerting to see so many doctors and nurses waiting in the room for me—like this was major surgery or something—but I quickly forgot about that when I glanced over at a partially hidden closet and saw some long, black, snake-like tubes hanging from hooks. The tubes looked long enough to stretch all the way to Russia. They were going to put one of those things up my what? But before I could rip out my IV and run for the hills, the anesthesiologist patted me on my shoulder and sent me off to La La Land with a delightful dose of Propofol, the infamous Michael Jackson drug.

Next thing I knew, some very kind nurses—more like angels, if I'm honest—gently woke me and asked if I'd like some coffee and graham crackers. I sat up like a seal and clapped my hands. Food! Food! Graham crackers had never tasted so good.

As soon as we got home, healthy and polyp-free, my husband and I raided the refrigerator. We didn't even shut the door—we just stood there in its light, snacking on lunch meat and cheese sticks, with the cool air hitting our faces.

When all is said and done, a colonoscopy is not a horrible or scary procedure. In fact, it should really be renamed the "colonoscopy diet"—the starvation and endless pooping caused both my husband and I to lose a few pounds. However, I do think there should be a souvenir presented at the end of the procedure, like "I survived a colonoscopy!" imprinted underwear.

Or maybe just a steak.

Call of Doodie

HAVE YOU EVER NOTICED how people become squeamish when the subject of bathroom habits comes up in conversation? I've attended cocktail parties where people have freely discussed birthing experiences, recent surgeries, and their children's latest bouts with projectile vomiting, but one mention of Irritable Bowel Syndrome? Suddenly everyone's clearing the room for a quick drink refill at the bar.

What's the big deal about grown-up poop? Why are so many people offended by the call of nature? Young mothers will eagerly discuss a baby's latest diaper blow-out, and everyone thinks it's adorable when "kaka" becomes one of the first words in a toddler's vocabulary. But once we get older, the subjects of one's poo consistency and frequency are suddenly taboo.

Pooping is by far the black (or shall we say brown?) sheep of the family when it comes to essential bodily functions such as eating, sleeping, and breathing. The ability to expel waste is just as vital to the human system as the ability to consume food—though admittedly, most of us would probably rather sit down to a five-star meal than sit down on a toilet. In fact, most people would expose their darkest family skeletons than admit to what goes on behind the bathroom door. Why?

In our family, it's pretty easy to determine who did what deed by whether or not the toilet overflows. Fortunately, when it does, a hearty plunging or two usually takes care of the problem. (I'm not going to lie—this is often a job that falls on my husband and is almost always punctuated by our children snickering outside the bathroom door as they watch him sweat and struggle with the rubber plunger.)

And what about families with bathrooms that have air freshener sprays strategically placed on back of their toilet tanks? What does that tell you about those families? We are the proud owners of two bathrooms, and both are equipped with a veritable arsenal of air fresheners.

Our family is unusually vocal about its poop habits too. We announce the urge when it strikes, and once the task has been completed, we exit the restroom with a full report on the project. Some members of my family will even go so far as to describe the nature of each poo, complete with explicit details on color, size, and consistency. Our all-time favorite? The mysterious corn poop. Just how long can a corn kernel linger inside the intestines?

Over the years, my parents and siblings have grown pretty well accustomed to my blunt observations on the subject of bowel evacuations, although my mother still shakes her head in disbelief when I joke about the mysteries of corn poop at the dinner table. My children are just as adventurous when it comes to their table conversations, but they've learned to curb their comments around certain company. This explains why we never serve corn on the cob when entertaining dinner guests. After an evening with my family, they'll never look at corn the same way again.

Gym Jerks

I'VE ALWAYS BEEN a sucker for those late-night, weight-loss info-mercials. As a result, I own an entire library of workout DVDs and a machine that transforms into a torturous, in-home gym. At first, I enjoyed exercising on my own schedule in the privacy of our home. I wore my ratty, satin shorts from the early 1990s, and didn't care if I looked like a Jane Fonda reject. But after a while, I got bored doing repetitive rounds of jumping jacks and yelling at the lady in pink tights on the TV screen.

As much as I dislike physical exertion, I can honestly say that I'm glad I ditched the DVDs in favor of my current membership at a women's gym. Now I actually look forward to my workouts — but this enjoyment comes at a price, and I'm not talking about the cost of a one-year membership. While most of the women at my gym are considerate, there are those who make the experience less than pleasurable:

Mirror Hogs. These are the women who run into class late and scoot to the front to get a spot by the mirror. Coincidentally, they're the same people who lack coordination and throw the entire class off.

Yappers. These ladies do not know when to stop talking. After living on rabbit food for a month, the last thing I want to hear about is your orgasmic experience with a seven-layer brownie cake.

Gym Poopers. These ladies drop their stink bombs off in the gym bathroom before hitting the treadmills. They need to do us all a favor and take their Milk of Magnesia AFTER they exercise.

DNA Swappers. Some people think nothing of leaving sweat puddles on the equipment, or hacking up a lung all over everything while recovering from the flu. DNA samples are NOT necessary— unless a forensics team wants to collect them after drawing your chalk outline on the gym floor.

Chronic Farters. These women have blowholes like whales and have no interest in corking them for the sake of other people's olfactory systems. When I walk into their fart clouds, my nose hairs feel singed, and my eyes water as if I've been hit with tear gas.

Exhibitionists. I don't understand women who come to the gym in shorts that scream "Cooch Alert!" and tank tops just begging for a Janet Jackson-style wardrobe malfunction. Go buy a damn bra.

Equipment Hogs. These people get lost in a daydream and sit for an hour on the machine instead of doing their reps. They make me wish I had a pocket defibrillator or Taser to shock them into moving.

Attention Seekers. You know the type. Surgically enhanced bodies and yet they whine, "Oh my gawd, I need to lose twenty pounds!" Just. Shut. Up.

The real heroes of the gym are the seventy-plus crowd of ladies still shaking their retired money makers in class. I admire their fortitude and hope to be just like them when I'm older. Flatulence and all.

My Love/Hate Relationship With Football

I LOVE THE FALL SEASON. The air is crisp, the leaves turn gold, the sweaters come out of storage, and pumpkin lattes abound. My husband loves fall for a different reason—football.

I've gone to more than my fair share of football games, and I've really tried to get into the sport. But the spirit just isn't there. If I go to someone's house to watch a game, I am far more interested in the finger foods than I am in whoever just scored a touchdown. I hardly ever remember who won the game, but I can tell you in detail every morsel I put into my mouth while watching it.

There are some benefits to the football season, however. When it kicks off in September, I immediately find myself needing extra yoga pants because my stomach instantly goes into "Expand-O-Matic" mode. In my house, football season is second only to the Christmas holidays for binge eating. It's the perfect excuse to act like the Romans did centuries ago—binge, purge, and gorge some more—and if you can't eat another bite? Just pretend you're a cow and switch over to your second stomach.

I love all of the personal time I get when football rolls around. While my husband turns into a football zombie for eighteen hours every weekend, I am at liberty to get completely and deliciously lost in the Internet Twilight Zone. Best of all, I can do it guilt-free, with no criticism from my husband over how much time I'm spending in front of a computer screen.

I'm also all smiles if the right team comes up victorious, because a win puts my husband in a good mood. It's the perfect time to call in favors, such as, "Honey, I need you to re-grout the bathroom floor," and "Babe, can we paint the house pink?" In the afterglow of a football victory, he'll do just about anything I ask—adopt another pug, host a ladies' book club meeting, or start up a sleep study camp for owls. If his team loses? My husband ends up in the worst of moods. Times like that call for breaking out the handy PEZ dispenser full of happy pills.

And while I may not be the biggest football fan of all time, who doesn't love the Super Bowl commercials? Normally, I hate television advertisements—I mute them or take a bathroom break. But when it's the Super Bowl, I'm glued to the set in anticipation of the funny commercials. Months down the road I won't recall who won the big game, but I'll still be an expert on E*TRADE talking babies, stomping Clydesdales, and those Dorito-eating dogs.

The final upside to the football season is my absolute favorite part—the drinking, which is synonymous with touchdowns, victories, and overtime. This year I plan on supplying Kegerator backpacks for my husband and all of his buddies, so that I don't have to be on call as barmaid during each game.

The downside to the season is that everything is scheduled around the games. Last year our lives revolved around the football calendar. We missed three weddings, two funerals, and the annual yard gnome convention. I'm also not crazy about all the screaming and cheering that goes on during the games. For sixteen weeks, I have to forgo my Sunday afternoon naps while my husband and his football pals are reduced to grumbling, hollering, clapping Neanderthals. They remind me of their caveman ancestors celebrating their latest kill around the campfire. Woolly mammoth wing dip, anyone?

At the very end of every football season, I do my celebratory dance as the time clock ticks down to zero. I grab the last chicken wing off the platter and smile—life is about to return to normal. Of course, that's when my husband cheerfully reminds me that basketball season is only six weeks away.

Gobble Be Gone

THANKSGIVING IS MY favorite holiday, a time when food addicts like me can guiltlessly consume mass quantities of calories in a twenty-four hour span. It's also the holiday for television chef wannabes to shine, and for food babies to be conceived. Families gather around the table to give thanks for their blessings, and then gather around the television to root for their favorite football teams. I love every bit of it, right down to my pilgrim salt and pepper shakers, and the handmade pinecone-turkey decorations from childhood.

It's the day AFTER the big holiday when all my thankfulness turns into regret. After overdosing on tryptophan, I wander around that next day in a food coma, unable to face the leftovers that are straining the capacity of my refrigerator. Forget finding the orange juice in there—it's hidden behind a turkey carcass and twenty Tupperware containers full of food. Each year, my husband insists on buying a turkey the size of an ostrich, whether we're feeding four people or forty, so it's up to me and Pinterest to figure out something clever to do with all that leftover meat. Turkey salsa? Turkey brownies? A turkey smoothie might do the trick for a quick jolt of liquid protein.

The side effects of Thanksgiving become apparent the minute I enter the bathroom. The scale actually winces when it sees me coming. Everyone knows that three pounds of holiday food is the equivalent of ten pounds on the scale. Why? Because stuffing inflates like dry cat food once it hits the stomach. I'm left feeling as puffed up as a Thanksgiving Day parade float. A quick glance in the mirror confirms my worst fears—I've become the very bird I consumed. At least it sure looks that way by the gobbler I'm sporting. It will take months of chin lifts to get rid of this sagging sucker.

I spend the majority of the day after Thanksgiving avoiding the very same family members I said grace with the night before. Grandma's creamed onion casserole has a way of repeating itself that no amount of perfume can conceal. The good news? I ate enough cranberries during the feast to stave off urinary tract infections for a year.

This is not a day for wearing sexy jeans. This is the day I pull out my old maternity pants and oversized sweatshirt with "Pilgrim Purge Party" printed on the back. It's also a good day to cozy up to a piece of pumpkin pie while watching an eight-hour long *Star Trek* marathon.

In the meantime, I'll be checking out Pinterest for turkey recipes and searching for cosmetic surgeons who can rid me of my gobbler.

Turkey martinis, anyone?

'Tis the Season

"IT'S THE MOST WONDERFUL time of the year!" Yeah, maybe it would be, if I kidnapped the Keebler Elves and forced them to do all of my shopping, wrapping, baking, and decorating. I could also use some foot massages along with a few hundred boxes of those fudgy cookies they're notorious for.

For us, the "season" officially starts after the last of the Thanksgiving leftovers are finished, including that gelatinous cranberry stuff that always ends up in the dog's bowl or someone's unlucky lunch box. It's at that point that my husband gets the urge to gas up the van and head for the Ozarks for a month of hibernation—just to avoid putting up the Christmas lights.

I'll admit it. I have a Christmas addiction. I probably need to attend meetings or some kind of support group, because I'm unable to pass a Hallmark store without stopping in for a quick purchase. This addiction has taken over my closets, my attic, and my husband's coveted tool shed. "You know you have a problem," he says every year. "You need help."

He's right. It's time I stood up at the local Holiday Hoarders Anonymous meeting and admitted the truth to the world: "Hello, my name is Marcia, and I'm a holiday hoarder."

Twenty-five rubber storage bins loaded with what my husband fondly refers to as "Christmas crap" are nestled under the rafters in our attic. Baby Jesus sleeps up there, right alongside Frosty the Snowman, Santa, and a wire reindeer with a bum leg. Something got into the attic last year and ate the Three Wise Men, but the way my husband sees it, that's one less box of crap to haul down from the attic. I honestly don't know why he complains so much—all he has to do is decorate our front lawn with thousands of LED lights so that it's bright enough to be seen by the International Space Station. Our power company sends us a thank-you note every holiday season.

Christmas lights always cause the worst issue with holiday decorating. Initially packaged in neat coils, they eventually become a tangled mess that NO ONE wants to deal with. It's also a mystery how they work fine one year when we pack them away. They continue to work fine the following year, when we take them out of the box and wrap them all over every tree, across the roof, and around the front windows of the house. They even work fine while we're standing back after we've finished, admiring the yard, doing a few high fives, and patting each other on the back for a job well done.

An hour later, only half of the strands of lights on the roof will still be lit, and the white icicles along the porch will suddenly flicker for a moment, gasp for breath, and fizzle out. Even the twinkling angel on the front lawn will get a droopy wing while the other wing will burn out completely. At that point, we have no choice but to return to Home Depot for more lights, but by then the pickings are slim. I don't want pink flamingo lights decorating the front of my house. The alternative is to purchase those giant lawn inflatables that look like Macy's Thanksgiving Day Parade rejects. At night they're not so bad—glowing and erect as if they've been given a big dose of Viagra, but come morning, after they deflate? They look more like fiesta-colored condoms strewn across the yard.

I'm the one who is always stuck doing the indoor decorations. It's just as bad as the outside decor. When the fiber optics craze was popular years ago, I collected every Santa, snowman, sled, elf, Christmas tree, and reindeer that sparkled, danced, and sang a cheery holiday tune. I also have an entire village of little porcelain houses that I know my husband would love to pillage. But what *really* drives him to drink gallons of spiked eggnog at this time of year are the cartons of decorations labeled "Assembly Required." On a particularly bad day, he'll claim that these boxes are grounds for divorce.

"Oh Christmas Tree, Oh Christmas Tree, How Steadfast Are Your Branches!" My husband doesn't think so. He breaks out in a sweat just contemplating the endless hours of affixing lights and delicate ornaments to sappy pine tree growth. So much so, in fact, that he convinced us to break tradition last year, switch to the dark side, and purchase a faux Christmas tree. Yes, that's right—I've got an artificial tree from China, not a real one from the mountains of North Carolina. The silver lining in all of this? No more pine needles to clog up the vacuum.

The worst part of my hoarding habit is my ornament collection. Hundreds—no, THOUSANDS—of them lie nestled in layers of crumpled tissue. When the ornaments come out, my husband gets that look in his eye like he'd rather dig a large hole in our back yard and tunnel his way to a warm island than spend the day decorating the tree with Bing Crosby, Perry Como, and our entire family. He is also terrified that history will repeat itself—I'm referring to the day we NEVER speak of—THE DAY THE TREE FELL DOWN. The day when all of my expensive, sentimental ornaments were reduced to glass shards scattered across a hardwood floor. Now we tie that sucker to the ceiling with endless loops of fishing line and guard it like it's Buckingham Palace.

Once the tree is up and the house is decorated inside and out, I'm forced to tackle the gift shopping list. This is my LEAST favorite part of Christmas. I'd much prefer to recline on the couch than wait in long lines at department stores at 3:00 a.m., when the zombies from *Night of the Christmas Living Dead* come out to feast. Maybe the store managers should offer people little cups of adult beverages while they wait in line. I bet no one would ever complain again.

The best part of the holiday is the party circuit that lasts several weekends in December. I start off the festivities in something sexy and black, with strappy little heels to match, but by the end of the month, buttons are popping off my clothes from all the alcohol and high calorie appetizers I've been grazing on for three weeks. I also end up swapping heels for bathroom slippers because my toes get permanently damaged from being jammed into stilettos every weekend.

As the twenty-fifth of December draws near, I'm forced to max out my credit card on Scotch tape, gift bows, and wrapping paper. By Christmas Eve, I've gone into frenzied gift-wrapping mode—sadly without the aid of the Keebler Elves. When Christmas Day actually arrives, I'm always dismayed by how quickly my house becomes cluttered with new toys, gadgets, and discarded paper. It took weeks to prepare for the big day, and within an hour, my home looks like a holiday battlefield.

The hardest part is taking everything down. I'm torn between relief at being able to dispense with all the holiday clutter and the desire to cling to the sentimentality of the season. But fitting everything back into the boxes from whence they came is the REAL challenge. Everything has to be disassembled, which requires an advanced degree in engineering that no one in my family has.

Once everything has been stored and the attic door closed, it's inevitable that we'll find a few stray items that were left behind in our weary state of packing. This means another trip to Walmart for more Rubbermaid containers. As I'm contemplating the aisles of Christmas decorations marked 50 percent off, my husband is contemplating divorce—or maybe just a conversion to Judaism. After all, how much room does a menorah take up?

Five Wishes for Santa

THERE ARE FIVE THINGS I'd like for Christmas, but I'm not going to visit the local mall and sit on some fat guy's lap with my wish list in hand. A candy cane and a pat on the head does not give me confidence that my Christmas wishes will be fulfilled. I'll just send a letter to the North Pole instead, and avoid the Santa lap dance and sticky candy cane groping.

I figure since I'm a middle-aged woman, I deserve more than one wish for Christmas. In my opinion, I've earned at least five:

1. I want to party like a rock star with the REAL Santa and his merry band of elves. But there are certain conditions. One, I am NOT cleaning up after those sloppy, drunk elves. Two, Santa MUST wear something other than that tiresome red suit. How about a kilt? Or maybe some jeggings. An industrial-strength girdle might even be in order after all the milk and cookies he sucks up on Christmas Eve like a Hoover vacuum.

2. I want to ride in a pimped-out sleigh with Santa, but only if there's a bottle of Cognac in the glove compartment. Rudolph won't be the only one with a red nose. Which reminds me—Santa needs to switch out that nose to an LED light to conserve energy.

3. I'd like to have my own reindeer. He could live in my back yard, and I could charge all the kiddies in the neighborhood admission for reindeer rides. He would also nibble on our grass during the spring, so we wouldn't have to mow the lawn as often.

4. I want all the elves to show up the day after Christmas to dismantle my holiday decorations and neatly pack them away in our attic. Ever notice how those lazy bastards suddenly disappear once the last gift has been unwrapped and the Christmas feast has been devoured? They don't even stick around long enough to help with the dishes.

5. I want to live in a world where acorn squash is high in fat and calories, and chocolate truffles are as nutritious as carrots. While you're at it, Santa, how about a gift certificate for a full body liposuction? Cookies in, cookies out. No more gingerbread on the thighs.

Sounds like the perfect wish list to me. Now hand over the reins and that bottle of Cognac, Mr. Claus!

The Holiday from Hell

CHRISTMAS 2001 WILL forever be known as The Season of the Neighborhood Flu Epidemic.

There is nothing worse than spending a major holiday like Christmas—a day that should be the biggest, most guilt-free binge fest of the year—with your head in the toilet. In such a situation, there is no cheerful clinking of champagne glasses, no surreptitious tasting of the gravy as it warms on the stove, no popping of sugar cookies in your mouth faster than an aardvark sucking up ants. There is only LONELY time in the bathroom contemplating the identity of the bright, confetti-colored items erupting from your stomach into the toilet bowl.

It is not a festive experience being a party of one, quarantined from family and friends like the town pariah, laying with your head pressed against the rim of the toilet and waiting for death. Swapping gifts on Christmas is fine. Germs, not so much. Sadly, the flu bug doesn't have discerning tastes and will happily descend upon any host it can find.

In 2001, we attended the annual neighborhood holiday party, traditionally held a few days before Christmas. As was customary, all of us on the block gathered for the festive event, to chat with old friends and strain the waistbands of our pants with an array of holiday foods. Little did we know that our stomachs and intestines were preparing to take us for a wild ride on the toilet train to hell.

There was a child at the party who was recovering from a recent bout of the flu, but none of us gave that a second thought as we chatted over rum balls and cheese dip. The party was a success and all of us left that night with full bellies and happy hearts. We had no clue that an invisible, uninvited guest had followed the majority of us home.

By Christmas Eve, the entire block was suffering from a nefarious flu bug, and it was taking us down one by one like dominoes. Yes, bubonic plague was alive and well in our neighborhood. The "Welcome to Our Home" plaque outside our front door should have been repainted to read: "Welcome to the Vomitorium."

While others were listening to "O Holy Night" and sipping apple cider, my oldest son and I were groaning "O Wretched Night," with a vomit bowl between us. It didn't matter that the stockings were not hung by the chimney with care, because old St. Nicholas would not soon be there. The ONLY thing that mattered to me was the sprinting distance between my mattress and the bathroom door. The problem was that I couldn't decide which end should hit the toilet first—my mouth or my backside. I compromised by sitting on the throne with the barf bowl in my lap to test out my multitasking skills.

That night we missed the candlelight Christmas Eve services at church, along with the big solo my son was going to perform with the choir. He was too busy making a casserole in the toilet to be bothered with hitting a few high notes. My husband was forced to pull quadruple duty with babysitting, gift wrapping, stocking stuffing, and the challenge of putting together both a doll house and a G.I. Joe command center.

On Christmas morning, I was greeted by the cheery sounds of more retching and moaning behind the bathroom door. My husband was down for the count, along with two more of our children. I knew it was a bad start to the day when no one raced into the living room to see what surprises Santa had left under the tree. The only surprise *I* wanted from Mr. Claus was another toilet, along with a stocking full of Pepto-Bismol and Kaopectate.

Once we reached four hours of vomit-free bliss, we felt well enough to attend the big family dinner at my parents' home. Selfish perhaps, but we were stir-crazy from staring into the depths of a toilet bowl for twenty-four hours, and we wanted to get out of the house. Taking into consideration that our motley crew evoked images of typhoid survivors, we did our best to control the contagious bug by refraining from bodily contact and by donning protective wear. At least the surgical masks and gloves made for some interesting Christmas family photos.

As we drove home that night and congratulated ourselves for surviving the holiday with our intestines intact, we heard the sound no parent ever wants to hear while they're behind the wheel of a car:

"Mommy? Daddy? I think I'm going to be sick!"

If we pretended not to hear our youngest daughter in the backseat, we were certain the specter of illness would surely disappear. But apparently Santa had other plans for us.

Is it any wonder why the following year there was a new porcelain throne under the Christmas tree with my name on it?

Rolling Out the New Year

I DON'T MAKE NEW YEAR'S resolutions because of the simple fact that I suck at keeping promises to myself. I'm great at keeping them for others, just not for myself. I could tell you plenty of stories of failed New Year's resolutions, and I even have the proof to show you: workout sneakers so heavily coated in cobwebs that they resemble giant cocoons (workout resolution fail); the anorexic bank account (savings resolution fail); and the moldy vegetables encrusted on the bottom drawer of my refrigerator (diet resolution fail). Just count the discarded McDonald's wrappers underneath my car seat and you'll quickly figure out how well I stuck to last year's weight loss goals.

I've decided to skip the whole resolutions thing this year so that twelve months from now, no one will be able to hold me to a bunch of empty promises. Instead, I'm going to list the things that I would LIKE to see happen, if I'm lucky enough to have the planets align in my favor. (Or if the Tooth Fairy, Santa Claus, and the Easter Bunny meet up at some kind of Wishes-R-Us seminar and decide to make me their poster child.) Maybe then these hopes and dreams of mine will come true:

Sleep. I need more of it. I'm tired of being shocked awake by the scary reflection that greets me in the bathroom mirror each morning. The dark circles under my eyes have me wondering if I'm sleepwalking into a boxing ring each night.

Exercise. I'm already a fan of any gym class with loud music and dancing, despite the fact that my dance moves aren't the only thing that's busting out. Think of two alley cats fighting in a burlap gunny sack, and that's a pretty accurate illustration of what's going on in my workout attire while I'm jumping around. Nevertheless, I'll continue to shake the generous portions of my body that God gave me, and maybe even attempt to add a little jogging to my treadmill routine. I might not be able to get out of bed for a few days afterwards, but at least it'll prevent me from wearing deeper grooves in the carpet from my mattress to the kitchen.

Less Hoarding. Hoarding animals, that is. Every year some orphaned creature ends up on my doorstep. There's a reason I have a Certified Wildlife Sanctuary sign posted in my front yard. This year my husband has decided to replace it with a new sign: "JUST SAY NO TO UNWED, PREGNANT RODENTS."

Libation Limitation. Okay, I've NEVER been able to stick with this goal, but it sounds good when I tell people that I'll try. I'm a firm believer that drinking should be limited to weekends and special occasions. The problem is that in my household, if all the picture frames have been dusted, that's a special occasion. A successful deworming session with the dogs? Special occasion. An argument-free dinner with my nineteen-year-old? Another special occasion. In short, I manage to find blessings each day that deserve a little celebration. "Pop open the champagne, Honey, I found the matching lids for every plastic food container in the house!"

Sugar Free. This is a really tough one to stick to. I love sweets and will eat just about anything covered in chocolate. Except insects. I'd rather chew on a toenail dipped in chocolate than eat something with six legs and a set of wings.

Less Internet Time. I need to spend less time on the computer and more time with my family. Facebook is an evil seductress who sucks me into hours of status updates, page lurking, and online conversations. Southern Cooking's website tempts me with glossy photos of food porn and recipes that are sure to add more pounds to the permanent, inflatable tire I call my waistline. My blog-stalking habit is akin to party-hopping at all my favorite friends' homes—the only thing missing is the wine. Then there are the numerous emails, which are a nuisance that bring out my OCD tendencies; each time my phone alerts me that a new email has arrived, I have to drop what I'm doing, read it, and then delete it to keep my inbox clutter-free. Too bad I don't have the same motivation when it comes to cleaning out my pantry.

Money Savings. This is another difficult one to stick to because of not-so-little things like car repairs, the kids' educations, weeping toilets, and ornery washing machines. Right now I have a dryer that screams like it's being tortured by wild banshees every time I throw a load of clothes into it. Chances are I'll need to buy a new one soon. There go my savings for that Elvis Presley Graceland plate collection I've been ogling.

There are plenty of other things I'm striving for in the New Year. I'd like to be more patient, less judgmental, more forgiving, and less moody. These are all admirable traits I need to work on, although it might be a bit of a challenge if I continue to deny myself sugar and libations. Still, I'm determined to look at the positive side of life from now on. In other words, I'm happy I'm not the one needing the deworming medication.

24/7 Pharmacy

MY MEDICINE CABINET looks like I spend my time burglarizing nursing homes and stockpiling the drugs in my bathroom. In addition to the necessities for curing a hangover (the three A's: aspirin, Alka-Seltzer, and Advil) and the creams that promise to de-wrinkle skin as leathery as a catcher's mitt, I also have a ten-year supply of vitamins and supplements on my shelves. In fact, there are so many vitamins that I have to use a second medicine cabinet just to fit them all in. I am a two-medicine-cabinet woman.

Every morning I lay out my pile of pills in a neat row, like little soldiers about to march into my gullet. Besides black cohosh for menopause, almost everything else is for heart health and my immune system. I'm pretty healthy—other than erratic mood swings and an appetite that could rival Genghis Khan's—but I'm also very paranoid. Which is why I take supplements to supplement my other supplements.

I collect every pill that Dr. Oz recommends to promote longevity—you name it, I've got it. Garlic pills, fish oil, flaxseed oil, magnesium, cinnamon, CoQ-10, Vitamin D, baby aspirin, and, of course, multivitamins. The problem is that I take them all at once, and about ten minutes later, I'm burping garlic cinnamon fish. These flavors do not mix well together, so after experiencing that unsavory taste in my mouth, I usually wash it all down with a cherry antacid and a cup of green tea. God only knows what that weird combination looks like in my stomach.

But it doesn't stop there. I take fiber supplements as well, and you know what THOSE are for.

My multivitamin promises to boost my energy level so that I can fold a month's worth of laundry in neat little squares, organize a box of Cheddar Bunnies, and do jumping jacks at 2:00 a.m. without needing a wink of sleep. So why are my eyelids drooping down to my chin every day after lunch? I had a crazy amount of energy before middle age set in — everyone used to ask if my morning coffee was administered through an IV drip, or just laced with amphetamines. Now that energetic young woman is more like a slug on sleeping pills. Forget one measly cup of coffee. I need to carry around the entire pot in a hip holster.

As if two medicine cabinets aren't enough, my husband and I have two more "special" drawers full of items. This is where all the gross stuff is hidden, just in case someone uses the bathroom and decides to root around in the medicine chest. No one wants to imagine one of us actually using these things, especially when that person isn't me. All of the most unpleasant tonics and tinctures actually belong to my husband. I'm talking about stuff like Gas-X, A+D Ointment, Lamisil, Imodium, Ben Gay, and Preparation H. Sounds like a party on the geriatric ward!

My husband also has weird tubes in that drawer — scary stuff that dates back to the early days of our marriage — even an enema kit with a picture of a smiling couple on the outside of the package. Who the hell smiles when they're about to have what looks to be a couples' enema?

Sometimes all the pills and ointments get confusing. Life can get interesting when I don't have my contacts in, or when my husband's glasses are nowhere to be found. I once squirted nail-strengthening serum into my eyes because the bottle looked similar to my eye drops, and my husband almost brushed his teeth with A+D Ointment. I guess that would keep his teeth from chafing! I wouldn't be surprised if he accidentally rubs toothpaste in all the wrong areas in a vain attempt to prevent rashes.

Another thing that confuses me is why people agree to take prescriptions with dangerous side effects. Medications such as these are frequently advertised on daytime television. Hair loss? Take this pill. Depression? Here's what you need. Severe indigestion? There's a pill for that, too. Overactive bladder? Erectile dysfunction? Nail fungus? Insomnia? Lots of pills for those. Then the commercials quickly spit out a list of countless side effects, veiled by some soothing music and a gorgeous, healthy couple playing Frisbee on the beach at sunset.

Why would anyone take a pill that could cause a stroke, heart attack, blurred vision, suicidal tendencies, hair loss, rashes, acne, or backed-up bowels? I don't want to wake up one morning bald with a third thumb growing out of my elbow. No thanks! I'll just stick to my supplements and catch the next bus out to the senior center.

Ready to Snap

IN THE PAST, I've been a pro at sidestepping conflict, but there comes a time in every woman's life when she just HAS to unleash the hormonal beast raging inside of her. I know that I personally get sick and tired of being stretched like a Gumby doll in ten different directions, all in some vain attempt to please the entire universe. Some days I'd rather just pull the covers over my head and staple them to the corners of my mattress.

Maybe I'm feeling this way because I'm menopausal and my hormones are running amok, or maybe I'm just older and wiser and I've finally realized I don't need to put up with everyone's crap anymore. My kids and my husband, I can handle. But if you're outside of that comfortable nucleus, and you see a sign taped to my front door that reads, "Beware! Enter at Your Own Risk," trust me. It's there for your own good.

Certain people REALLY frustrate the hell out of me. I'm particularly annoyed by those who shove their political agendas down my throat via emails, robo-calls, television ads, bulk mail, and Facebook. I find them especially insulting if the political onslaught hits me early in the morning, when my eyes are still at half-mast. I'm basically brain dead until 9:00 a.m.—when the coffee kicks in—so if you ask me to support your politician's campaign before then, I may just end up voting for SpongeBob.

There are also those clueless people who have a special talent for hijacking check-out lines. I am not a happy camper when, after I've waited for twenty minutes in the "Ten Items or Less Express Lane" at the grocery store, I discover that some joker in front of me a) has fifteen items in his basket, including eight cans of corned beef hash, six jars of pickled pigs' feet, and a ginormous bag of dog food; b) has discovered he can't afford that many jars of pickled pigs' feet and needs the check-out girl to de-scan them all; and c) attempts to pay for his purchases with an expired credit card. Shoppers like him make me snarl and gnash my teeth.

People who play the "poor me" card also drive me to distraction. They can't pay their mortgages but they somehow scrape up the funds to take weekend getaways at the beach, drive BMW convertibles, and suck down lobster tails at five-star restaurants. They need to rethink their priorities.

Delayed service callouts are another source of angst for me:

Dear Mr. Internet/Television/Telephone/Electricity
Repair Man,

I don't mind sitting in a dark cavern for two weeks
waiting for you to show up and restore our service.
I'll just sit here in the candlelight and crochet a pastel
noose while I wait patiently for your visit.

Love, Marcia

People who talk about me or my family behind my back instantly turn me from Glenda the Good Witch into the Wicked Witch of the West. Criticize my kids, and I'll go Charlie Sheen on your ass. Yes, I know my children have done some stupid things over the years, but I'm pretty sure your kids have done the same. Stop judging. This is not a competition. Don't make me get my broom out.

I feel much the same way about people who try to involve me in the "he said, she said" game. I'm done playing referee and would much rather sit along the sidelines while the two of them duke it out. There's plenty of popcorn to go around.

Erratic drivers who multitask behind the wheel while speeding down a busy interstate are another trigger. These people can't be human—they're clearly aliens from a planet inhabited by octopus people. It amazes me how they can text, apply makeup, slip a contact in their eye, and brush their teeth, all while dodging in and out of traffic.

I'm also annoyed by celebrities who whine about their lack of privacy and their constant run-ins with the paparazzi. After all those years clawing their way to the top, what did they expect? If it's so terrible, they can always switch careers. "Hey Biebs, I hear they're hiring janitors at the local middle school." No need to worry about paparazzi showing up there.

Next up on the irritation scale are door-to-door salesmen. It never fails—we'll be just sitting down to dinner when the doorbell will ring and some questionable-looking guy who looks hyped-up on meth is there trying to sell me an alarm system, magazine subscription, or set of Ginsu knives. The only salespeople that I allow to cross my threshold are the ones selling Girl Scout cookies or those giant chocolate bars whose proceeds go to support the high school glee club.

Other people who get on my last nerve are the ones who brag about their high-paying jobs, yet bitch about the lengthy hours they put in each week. They actually believe that the rest of us poor slobs do nothing but sit around the pool all day and sip piña coladas. Who do they think they're kidding? Just stop. Everyone knows they're the ones keeping TLC, MTV, and the Bravo Channel afloat by never missing an episode of *16 and Pregnant*, *Real Housewives of New Jersey*, and *Toddlers & Tiaras*.

I'm actually not sure what type of person is worse—the people who brag about money or the cheapskates. Don't wrap the Family

Dollar "Wine Special of the Week" in fancy trimmings and bring it to our cocktail party when I know damn well you can afford the good stuff. You can wrap your trash up in a pink bag with purple bows and it's still gonna smell like crap to the garbage man.

These are the types of people who have been sucking the life out of me for years. To heck with them. Now it's time for me to kick back, pour a glass of wine, and watch back-to-back episodes of *Koalas Gone Wild*.

The Seven Deadly Sins of Menopause

WE ALL HAVE THEM — the secret sins that keep us awake at night and tap us repeatedly on the shoulder during the day. They're the sins that we would prefer our friends and neighbors never know about. For some, these indulgences include dancing the salsa naked with a Swiffer mop (I didn't say that was me). For others, they include gorging on a bag of bite-sized, cheese-flavored rice cakes at 2:00 a.m. (okay, maybe that one *was* me).

I'm not Catholic, but I might as well be sitting in a confessional booth right now, because I'm about to spill the goods on the seven deadly sins of menopause:

Envy. I live near a park with a jogging trail. I see women of all ages out there, rollerblading, running, and biking. Certain ones catch my eye — the PERFECT ones, who look like they just rolled off of the Barbie shelf at Target. The ladies in pink sweats with the Juicy Couture label stretched tight across their firm, little butts. The women in matching tank tops pulled taut across breasts that don't jiggle like JELL-O cups in a truck when they jog. THOSE are the ones I envy. They're blessed with perky boobs that look to the sky instead of their knee caps. Their pre-baby bodies are free of the endless trails of stretch marks that so closely resemble the NYC subway system. They can still do every yoga position. All of it makes me long for my youth and a certain pink bikini I once wore.

Gluttony. This is the reason I no longer wear the aforementioned pink bikini. I am an acknowledged wine hoarder and cake pop connoisseur. I'm also extremely selfish with take-out food. To prevent my kids from stealing my leftovers, I remind them that in certain cultures, thieves get their hands chopped off as punishment for such crimes. This helps keep my food-filching teenagers away from my stash while I'm busy searching the Internet for more cake pop recipes.

Pride. This is something easily lost when you›re driving a rundown car with missing hubcaps and a broken door handle. And it's precisely the reason why you'll NEVER see me behind the wheel of our ancient family automobile, with its tendency to seize up at every stoplight in town. It's also the reason I never look in a full-length mirror anymore—I can't handle seeing all of my body parts wiggling and waving back at me in that unnatural way.

But if you ask me about my kids or granddaughter, I'll whip out my cell phone faster than you can say "moo shu pork" and force you to watch a terminally long slide show of every phase in their lives, starting with their ultrasound images and ending with their college graduation ceremonies.

Lust. When you're menopausal, the mind says "Yes" to sex but the body says, "Oh, hell no!" So you learn to lust after other things instead, like an overstuffed quesadilla the size of a Pomeranian. Or Ben & Jerry's Triple Caramel Chunk ice cream and a bottle of Dom Pérignon. A trip to Tahiti would be nice, too, but at this rate, I'll never fit into that pink bikini again.

Anger. Think Jack Nicholson in *The Shining* or Anthony Hopkins in *The Silence of the Lambs*. I become as furious and deranged as psychos like these when my son misses the school bus at 6:30 a.m. My head has been known to spin like I'm in the throes of an exorcism when my husband, dispatched to the hardware store for a socket set, returns with a singing can opener.

Sloth. When I contemplate the sin of sloth, the first image that comes to my mind is one of Jabba the Hutt. No, I'm *not* saying I resemble a bloated, slug-like alien, or that I eat fleshy, wriggling creatures with slimy legs. But I DO like being surrounded by min-ions (a.k.a. children) that can take out the trash, wash the dishes after dinner, and tidy up rooms that look like they've just been hit by a tornado.

Greed. While most people associate greed with money and power, neither of these things appeals to me. No, I'm greedy when it comes to sleep—precious, precious sleep. Those evil menopausal twins, Hot Flash and Fatigue, often join forces with their mischie-vous cousin Insomnia to deprive me of my solid seven hours of slumber. (Never one to miss a party, my bladder is right there with them, shaking and grooving till the break of dawn.) If there really is such a thing as reincarnation, I want to come back as a bear so I can hibernate for a few months, then bite the head off the first person who wakes me.

I realize that the deadly sins are always seven in number, but when it comes to menopause, there's an eighth sin that deserves an Honorable Mention—the sin of LUNACY. When my body thermo-stat mirrors the mercury level of an Arizona summer, or I suddenly find myself canvasing the girdle aisle at Save Mart, I'm bound to go a little crazy. To combat the bipolar urges I feel due to my wildly fluctuating hormones, I've discovered that the road to happiness is paved with Prozac and chocolate—and maybe a side trip to Tahiti with my pink bikini in my suitcase.

Easy Does It

EVERY SUMMER MY Facebook news feed is besieged with vacation photos of friends and family members. It drives me crazy! There they all are—jet skiing on a lake in North Carolina, hiking in Colorado, and zip-lining through forests in West Virginia. And here I am, sitting at my computer and nibbling on a chocolate chip cookie.

As I scroll through these pictures, I wonder: "HAS THE WORLD GONE MAD?" I don't want to spend my vacation under a blistering sun in the Grand Canyon—I can close my eyes during some particularly intense night sweats and pretend I'm already there. Who wants to jog six miles around a serene lake in Tennessee? I don't—not unless I'm being mugged or chased by a creepy, knife-wielding circus clown. And why would I want to spend an entire day peddling along a bike path, dodging pebbles and pinecones, feeling my ass grow numb on a hard plastic seat?

Every summer when I was young, my parents would transform into wandering nomads, hungry for adventure and eager to get away from the daily grind. What did this mean for me, exactly? It meant cramming ten pounds of my crap into a four-pound suitcase and being sandwiched between three other sweaty, belligerent teenagers in the back seat of a rental car.

These long road trips led to some "interesting" experiences, which I'm convinced is why I need anti-anxiety medications today: walking down spider-infested trails through a citrus grove; sleeping on a freezing mountaintop in a tar paper shack with no heat, bathroom, or running water; vomiting over the side of a boat during a fishing trip on rough water (my brother later referred to this as "making homemade chum"); and sleeping by myself in the backseat of our rental car because my siblings convinced me there were nuclear-reactor-sized scorpions under my cabin bed in Zion National Park.

My parents' idea of communing with nature involved long hikes through mountainous territory with their children huffing and puffing behind them (okay—maybe that was just me, struggling for oxygen). Sometimes, if I got lucky, these strenuous, test-your-endurance-type trails involved horseback riding. This was preferable to me, since the horse did all the sweaty labor while I just sat back in the saddle and did some serious daydreaming.

It was inevitable that my sloth-like attitude toward vacations would catch up to me as an adult. While my husband and children would tube down water slides or head out for some deep sea fishing, I would spend my vacation time enjoying leisurely brunches, with nothing on my schedule but museum tours and late-afternoon naps. Sadly, I could only get away with this routine for so many years. Before long, some close friends of ours convinced us to rent a cabin for a week in the woods. No television or Internet—just a lake, and miles of miles of nature trails.

I came prepared—with a grocery sack full of paperbacks and magazines. I snuck a few bags of chocolate in there as well, in case a menopausal meltdown occurred and I needed to self-medicate. (My husband has learned a long time ago to keep emergency chocolate on hand at all times. A menopausal woman who is hot, thirsty, and hungry is *much* more dangerous than an ornery grizzly bear in Yellowstone National Park.)

For the most part, it was an enjoyable trip. I survived the long trails, the relentless mosquitoes, and the pitch-black evenings filled with unidentifiable animal sounds. It wasn't until our last full day at the park that I realized how woefully inept at outdoor activities

I really am. Our friends decided it was a fine day for canoeing, and there was no longer any plausible excuse for me to escape the adventure that my family so readily embraced.

EVERYONE in our group had been canoeing at least once in their life—except for me, but I was damned if I was going to admit it. After all, how hard could it be? I had seen several other mothers paddling down the river in a kayak just the day before, so I figured there was no reason I couldn't be Pocahontas for a day and give canoeing a whirl.

After a clumsy attempt at dragging a canoe down to the river, my daughters and I hopped into the boat and began paddling. Actually, they did all the paddling, while I sat in the middle like a queen bee and wondered if beverages were going to be served on this little river excursion. Never mind that there were signs posted all along the riverbank warning us to BEWARE OF ALLIGATORS! And never mind that the combination of weight between the three of us had caused the canoe to dip precariously low in the water. Tourists did this every day, so I figured it had to be safe.

Ten minutes into our trip, I realized the scenery hadn't changed much. Same trees, same dock, same people waiting for canoes and snickering at us. Apparently, my daughters had forgotten everything they'd learned in Canoeing 101, and our canoe was spinning counterclockwise on the water like a toy sailboat circling a drain. Water began seeping into the sides of the boat, and all I could think of was the sprinting distance between our miniature Titanic and dry land (assuming I could do the walk-on-water thing), and whether or not I had updated my will to provide for my pet chinchillas.

Somehow we made it back to shore, and I swore never to park my fanny in another canoe for as long as I lived. Unlike Pocahontas, I would never see what was just around the river bend, and I had no desire to. All I cared to see at that moment was the bottom of a martini glass.

I've since learned that, for me, a vacation is not about eating like a sparrow and working out like an Olympic hopeful. It's about sleeping late on sheets made of Egyptian cotton, and stretching out on a sunny beach with a piña colada in one hand and a bestselling novel in the other. It's about ordering Maine lobster without looking at the price, and letting your hands get sticky from a melting ice cream cone. It's about catching fireflies in jars, and telling ghost stories around a campfire until everyone is too afraid to crawl back into their tents to go to sleep.

Next summer, the only vacation pictures I'll be posting for friends will be of me lounging in a fold-up chair at an outdoor concert—or sipping some fruity concoction under a palm tree.

On the Road Again

I'VE BEEN KNOWN to go bonkers when confined to a car for hours on end. The boredom and lack of space cause me to keep my eyes constantly peeled for the nearest roadside bar. I lose all feeling in my butt, my long legs ache from being folded up like an accordion under the dash, and my constant fiddling with the A/C leaves the rest of my family members shivering or sweating to death in the backseat.

There are a lot of issues that make me want to claw my way out of the car during a long road trip, and the radio is at the top of my list. One minute I'm listening to Bon Jovi and digging it, then the radio station changes in the next city, and suddenly Tony Bennett is serenading me with a love ballad that makes me want to stick a fork in my eye. Another hour on the road, and Toto's "Africa" comes on, which prompts the bored men in the car to break out in song—and that's when I feel like I'm trapped on a tour bus with the Vienna "Sour Note" Boys' Choir.

Mindless snacking also takes over on these extended trips. Long hours in the car cause terminal boredom, and we all know that boredom breeds hunger. And that means that every five minutes, I'm popping handfuls of Cheez-Its and Milky Way bites into my mouth like a whacked-out snack addict. I might as well forget all about the skinny jeans I've got crammed into my suitcase.

Along with the unhealthy amounts of snacks we eat on the road, we're always in a big rush to get to our destination, which means food from drive-through restaurants becomes a staple of our traveling diets. Junking out on fast food while driving 80 miles per hour down the interstate is never fun, especially if there are no napkins on hand. Half of the food ends up in our laps, and the rest of it on our greasy chins. By the time we emerge from the car at our final destination, we look like we've just played paintball with ketchup, mustard, and chocolate milkshakes.

Needless to say, all of this food gets washed down with gallons and gallons of various beverages. Consequently, my bladder knocks at the door non-stop:

"Hello? Remember that iced coffee you insisted on chugging down seventy miles ago?"

"Hey there, it's that super-sized Diet Coke you had about thirty miles back."

"Look. I know you want to finish that bottle of water you're working on, but THERE IS NO ROOM LEFT. GO PEE!"

Of course, Murphy's Law inevitably kicks in at this point, and traps me in the middle of bumper-to-bumper traffic on the interstate. This is when I place my hands together in silent prayer: "Dear Bladder, I know I have taken you for granted during this car trip, but please ... don't fail me now." It's also when I'm forced to consider using my red Solo cup for something other than it was designed for. (In all fairness, the cup is probably cleaner than most of the highway rest stops we visit. Then again, where else can you get a soda for five bucks, a bag of chips that expired two months ago, and a packet of boiled peanuts from a one-armed man?)

Eating all that crappy fast food and sitting for hours on our rear ends has the added side effect of filling the car with noxious fumes. It's a job that those little pine-scented tree-shaped air fresheners just cannot handle. I try to suffocate myself with a pillow when my husband and son play "Dueling Farters."

Once we reach our destination, the real adventure begins. Our hotels are never like the Beverly Wilshire. I'm not sure where the majority of hotel chains purchase their pillows, but I'm betting they buy them from sandbag factories. The mattresses are no better. They're so hard that I wake each morning folded over like an elderly man with rheumatoid arthritis.

Six of us sharing one hotel bathroom can keeps things interesting, especially if we've indulged in the all-you-can-eat Chinese buffet the night before. The managers would be wise to install timers in each bathroom so that everyone can get their fair share of privacy on the stink throne. Large bath towels would also be a very welcome addition. It's impossible to dry off properly with a towel the size of a dinner napkin.

I'd also like to suggest to hotel management that foam padding be added to the walls of every hotel room, so that guests don't have to listen to the over-amorous honeymooners next door, the loud family upstairs with the screaming toddler, and the news crew filming the prostitution sting down the hall.

In spite of all these inconveniences, would I do a road trip with my family again? Absolutely. The moments of deep laughter that cause our eyes to water and our bellies to ache are worth every mishap. But next time, we'll skip the buffet—and make sure to pack a bottle of Gas-X, just in case.

Aviation Traumatization

I DON'T FLY—ever—but I used to. I come from a family of avid travelers, and I grew up with parents who, for some sadistic reason, thought it would be fun to drag four kids to a different national park each summer by way of a jumbo jet. While my siblings enjoyed these journeys through the friendly skies, I was the anxious kid popping Dramamine pills like Tic Tacs before boarding a flight. I learned at an early age to control my fears and my sphincter muscles just enough to avoid any unexpected, embarrassing accidents in Row 15.

By the time I married, I was a seasoned flyer. It still gave me a nervous stomach, but at least I was no longer white-knuckling a barf bag during takeoff. Things changed once my kids were born. I started questioning that pesky mortality thing, and began harboring an irrational fear that my babies would end up motherless, like Bambi. It didn't help that I was a sucker for television reports on airplane crashes, and that my phobia had become validated after a few hair-raising experiences of my own. Now no amount of Xanax or alcohol will get me back up in the skies.

My fear of flying has been compounded by the mystery of the Bermuda Triangle, a corner of which is only a mile off the coast of where I live. Many flights out of Fort Lauderdale circle over this mysterious patch of the Atlantic Ocean, where dozens of planes have fallen off the radar and disappeared. There's a reason it's nicknamed the Devil's Triangle, and the idea of becoming fish food or part of an *Unsolved Mysteries* episode just doesn't appeal to me. I prefer to think those planes detoured through the *Twilight Zone* and arrived on *Gilligan's Island.*

Beyond the frightening takeoff and landing aspects of flying, the plane itself is a claustrophobic's nightmare. Being herded like cattle into a steel contraption that resembles a giant MRI tube is not my idea of fun—nor is fitting my ass into one of those narrow seats, then needing the Jaws of Life to get it back out. Furthermore, would it be so hard for the oxygen masks to drop down automatically whenever someone farts on a flight? It also wouldn't hurt for every overhead bin to be equipped with a mini bar, for the relaxation of fearful flyers.

Airplane bathrooms are another issue to contend with while flying forty-five thousand feet in the air. Forget being inducted into the Mile High Club—every time the plane hits a pocket of turbulence and drops what feels like a few hundred feet, so do my bowels. I also have an irrational fear that if I sit too long on an airplane toilet, my derrière will get sucked out into the stratosphere.

The only way you're going to coax me onto a flight today is if you promise me a bottle of rum and a first class seat next to Johnny Depp. If the plane nosedives into the Devil's Triangle, hopefully I'll at least be transported to *Gilligan's Island.* If you need to find me, I'll be the one sipping piña coladas in the tiki hut with Jack Sparrow.

My Father's Chair

THE SOFT PADDED chair envelopes me in memories of my father; the leather is worn where his arms once rested. I run my fingers over the smooth patches to get a sense of him, and breathe deep the scent of leather and success. From this chair, my father managed a real estate and banking business, arranged our summer vacations to the Southwest, and designed his dream home in Montana. His legacy is now tucked away in the cardboard boxes that surround me, his voice a distant echo against these bare walls.

Packing up his office, I find a grainy, black-and-white photo that sparks memories of a man who carried me on his shoulders in the pool, made me laugh with his Cookie Monster imitations, and, when I was older, shared his quiet wisdom with me on a porch in Whitehall, Montana.

The world remembers him as a successful entrepreneur who was larger than life—an intense man of intellect, integrity, and power, who enjoyed a lifelong pursuit of excellence. To me, he was just Dad. He was the man who was my shelter in a world of uncertainties. No matter my age, I was always his little girl.

At times, he was imposing and strict, reprimanding me when I tested the limits of his patience. Like any teen, I resented his advice until I had children of my own, and came to understand that the boundaries he set for me were always rooted in love. But there was also a softer side to my father that few people knew. He could be moved to tears when listening to a Wagner opera or the complexities of a Mahler symphony. His eyes misted over whenever he expressed his love and gratitude for my mother. And he hugged us tightly, as if he never meant to let go. When I close my eyes, I can still feel his arms around my shoulders and the soft fabric of his shirt against my cheek.

When my father was first diagnosed with blood cancer, there was no doubt in my mind that this powerful man would beat the disease. We had spent an entire summer together tracing his ancestral roots and discovered that longevity was in his family genes.

He fought the good fight with chemotherapy, but the insidious cancer robbed him of all the simple joys in life. The gourmet food and wine he once loved now tasted like cardboard. He battled daily against nausea and fatigue. It was difficult watching a man who was once so active in sports, and such a strong force in the boardroom, become thin, fragile, and confused. I couldn't accept that he was being defeated, even as the soft angles of his face were sharpened by rapid weight loss and exhaustion. But the day I embraced him and could feel the knotted rope of his spine against my fingertips, I realized that the cancer was winning. He no longer had the strength to hug me back.

My father spent his last days in hospice care with his family surrounding him. I remember how his eyes lit up when we walked into the room, and I can still feel his feeble attempt to squeeze my hand as I sat beside him on the bed. Choking back tears, I spoon-fed him his dinner and reminisced about happier times. Looking back, we should have played Wagner or Mahler to soothe him, but I like to think the music was there nonetheless, playing in his dreams and lulling him to sleep.

We lost him two weeks before Father's Day. I pressed my face against his chest like I did as a child, and this time I heard the last beat of his heart.

My father had always been my idol, and the inspiration that drove me to succeed. He saw the potential in the humorous stories

I wrote and encouraged me to become the writer I am today. He believed in me when I was unable to believe in myself, and he pushed me to heights unimaginable. I miss his humor and the deep chuckle that resonated in his voice when he regaled us with tales from his youth. I miss our summer vacations, family holidays, and the laughter we shared over a good bottle of wine. But most of all, I miss his strong embrace.

I feel him now in the threads of Mahler's music and the stories I write from the comfort of his brown leather chair. When I look to the west, I see his smile beyond the darkness, a shooting star that leaves a bright trail across the summer night.

If He Were a Rich Man

MY HUSBAND AND I LOVE to fantasize about what we would do if we ever won millions of dollars in the state lottery. This question is a no-brainer for me—I'd pay off my debts and donate a large portion of the remainder to cancer research. But the whimsical side of me would also donate to a home for abandoned squirrels and use some money to create an organization called "Bears, Badgers, and Beavers without Borders."

One time, when we were contemplating this conundrum over martinis on the front porch, my husband's tongue began to loosen up significantly with each sip of gin. That's when I found out exactly what my guy would do with a cool million.

Before we take this story any further, there's something you should know about the other half of my marriage equation: my husband is a wannabe inventor. Most of his ideas are so far out there that they are beyond comprehension, but sometimes I see that flash of brilliance in his eyes, and I know he's onto something unique. Or scary.

Here's what my husband would do with a million dollars:

- Invent tequila-laced ice packs for hot-flashing menopausal women.
- Create "testosterone teddy bears." Men would sleep with them and wake up as hairy as bears.

- Invest in latex underwear. They would be leak-proof and would never get holes ripped in them from excessive sharting.
- Build affordable army tanks for easy travel. You'd never have to worry about speeding tickets, door dings, or expensive tire replacement. Each tank would also come equipped with a toilet and well-stocked mini bar.
- Invent an automatic underarm-hair braider for men. It would alleviate the pain of armpit hair being yanked out at the roots by roll-on deodorants.
- Start a new support group, "Burpers Anonymous," for chronic burpers. This would be a safe haven where people could burp freely without judgment. Carbonated beverages and spicy black-bean queso dip would be served at every meeting.
- Invent donkey-fur toilet paper so that people could stop making asses out of themselves.
- Create a robotic beer butler that would carry a mini keg on its back at all times, with a tap at your disposal.
- Start a chain of zip-line courses that stretch across giant shark tanks, just to make things more interesting.
- Open an underwater golf course. Instead of golf clubs, you would use spear guns with balls attached to the ends of them. No need for special golf attire—you'd wear a wet suit and fins. It would become a competitive sport in the Olympics known as "Snorkel Golf."

I think it's time to hide the gin and slip my husband some Lunesta. Once he's snoring, I'll take off with our theoretical millions, open a squirrel orphanage in Cancun, and hang out on the beach with a bottle of sunscreen in one hand and a tequila ice pack in the other.

Devil Juice

MY HUSBAND IS AN AVID beer drinker, but when he switches over to wine (or as he calls it, "Devil Juice"), he becomes a different person with drastically different moods. When he uncorks his second bottle of red wine, I never know *which* alter ego I'm going to be dealing with—Cuddle Bear, Sleepy the Dwarf, or Crabass McBastard. One thing I do know for sure is that none of these personalities will remember a thing in the morning. Because when my husband is in a Devil Juice haze, he could paint the house, wax the car, install new plumbing, or dance around the fire pit wearing a cat mask and singing the Meow Mix theme song—he won't have the slightest memory of any of it the next day.

My spouse claims that Devil Juice alters my personality, too. He says I go from lamb to lion to human Gummy Bear after only a few glasses of vino. This has encouraged me to buy cheaper wine and dilute it with ice water—it's gross, but we can't have two comatose adults roaming around the backyard, can we? Or worse, one comatose adult and one dancing man in a cat mask.

Years ago, our family owned a gift basket shop, and we were fortunate enough to come across caseloads of good quality champagne at a discount price from a local wine dealer. Most of the bottles ended up in our kitchen cabinets instead of the baskets they were intended for. A close friend of ours even bought several cases and nicknamed it "forget-me-not" Champagne since she woke up each morning with no memory of what she had done the night before. It's true that wine comas rob you of chunks of time you can never get back, until one day you stumble across yourself crawling around on all fours in a YouTube video.

Sometimes, after enough glasses of Devil Juice, my husband becomes convinced he's the next Iron Chef. He fixes weird sandwiches like bologna with garlic croutons, or peanut butter and jelly with roasted turkey. Then he tries to talk everyone else into eating these creations, and trust me when I say that Guy Fieri he is not.

I'll admit that sometimes vino turns me into a Top Chef as well. Some of my tastiest concoctions have been created after downing a few glasses of Devil Juice. The next day I may not remember what I ate the night before, but I know it must have been good, because zipping up my jeans is impossible.

You would think two middle-aged adults would not want to lose track of precious time by blurring their weekends with Devil Juice. There's just something not right about a man in a cat mask drinking wine. Next weekend he's changing his own litter box.

In-Laws from Hell

WHEN YOU MARRY your significant other, there should be something written into the vows about the inheritance of family baggage. Before the ink is even dry on the marriage certificate, some of your in-laws will already be morphing into outlaws, armed and ready to rob you of your newly wedded bliss.

These people are notorious for sucking the joy out of every family event and gathering. Holidays and celebrations bring out the worst sides of their personalities, causing everyone to drink more, socialize less, and spend an inordinate amount of time hiding in the bathroom. Sure, there are some people out there who have wonderful relationships with their in-laws; however, more often than not, there's at least one particular relation who loves to stir the pot and share his or her cup of misery.

You know you have a potential problem if you've got in-laws who fall into any of the following categories:

The Attention Seekers. Everything in their lives is far more stressful (and far more important) than anything in yours. They work longer hours, have busier schedules, and never have time to relax. Warning: if you are a stay-at-home-mom, this type of in-law believes you do nothing all day but read trashy novels and eat bonbons in bed.

The Drama Queens. These people thrive on family drama. They're usually unhappy, insecure, and pushy people who enjoy dragging you down their emotional rabbit holes. Whatever stunt they pull at the next family function is sure to be a showstopper.

The Overbearing Parents. These in-laws feel that their precious offspring could easily have married someone better than you. Your housekeeping and parenting skills will never measure up to their royal standards. You and your kin will always be considered mere serfs in their kingdom—but don't bother polishing any crowns, because chances are you'll never get the chance to wear one.

The Gossipers. These parasitic in-laws are worse than any flu bug that might ever inhabit your intestines. They suffer from diarrhea of the mouth and love to watch the poop hit the fan when they bad-mouth you to vulnerable family members who are easily manipulated by their crock of dung. Poo-Pourri will never be necessary for these people, because they're convinced their poop doesn't stink.

The Competitors. Like territorial alley cats, these in-laws treat you like an intruder and feel they can best you at anything. They turn everything into a competition, always making sure you're aware that they live in better neighborhoods, own larger homes, and drive more expensive vehicles. They'll brag about their salaries, their latest vacations, their new wardrobes, and their child's latest report cards. While they're busy reminding you how beautiful and special they are—and how much weight they've lost— just keep in mind they're doing all of this in order to mask the mind-boggling amount of insecurities that fester inside them.

In the old Wild West, outlaws were shot on sight. In today's society, the only ammo we have is patience, understanding, and forgiveness.

I vote we step back in time.

Here Comes Peter Cottontail

EVERY CHRISTIAN ADULT knows that Easter is all about Jesus and the Resurrection, but for most kids it all comes down to one thing—chocolate bunnies. I've never understood how rabbits got mixed into the story of the Resurrection, but every spring there are rows and rows of chocolate bunnies on the grocery store shelves, their colorful, candy eyes staring out from cellophane wrappers.

Worse than the bunnies are the chocolate crosses with marzipan lilies wrapped around the base. I don't think that's what God had in mind for us when it comes to celebrating Easter.

If you're only into the holiday for the gastric pleasure, then you understand how complicated buying Easter candy can be for the consumer. It's almost impossible to find simple chocolate eggs these days. Today, every popular brand of candy offers eggs with every filling imaginable. Even stranger are the jelly beans with exotic flavorings like buttered popcorn, Coca-Cola, and something that tastes like charcoal. Who wants to eat candy that tastes like the stuff you scrape off the bottom of your grill?

The Easter candies I've never been fond of are marshmallow Peeps. These "treats" come in all different shapes: bunnies, ducks, eggs, and crosses. My husband claims they taste better if they sit out on the kitchen counter for days and "age" like a fine wine. I remind him that five-star restaurants don't serve stale marshmallows for a reason.

My youngest son has a completely different way to enjoy his Peeps. He likes to stick them in a microwave and watch them grow. They swell up like giant sponges until they look like they're about to start breathing on their own. It makes you wonder what happens to them in your stomach once you've eaten a few. I imagine there are elderly people across the country with the residue of yellow Peeps still stuck to the sides of their colons.

When I was a child, my mother would hide all of our Easter candy throughout the house, and hunting for it was the one time of the year that I actually attempted to compete with my older siblings. Sadly, fearing that their children would slip into a diabetic coma from sugar overload, my parents always confiscated our baskets after we did all the hard work of filling them up. They would then proceed to dole out small portions of candy each night after dinner.

On one particular Easter, I was completely traumatized when my mother handed me a giant, chocolate bunny—a bunny that I discovered later was hollow inside—a "cheater bunny." It left me wondering if the manufacturer had created these "special" bunnies to save money or to encourage chubby kids like me to consume less chocolate. Either way, it seemed like a cruel joke to play on an eight-year-old.

As a little girl, I swore that when I had children, they would be the masters of their own Easter baskets. I held true to my word and for years did my best to make sure each Easter was a memorable holiday for the family. Even now that my children are in their late teens and mid-twenties, if they're home for Easter, they have to participate in an egg hunt. (Their priorities have changed, however. It's not the chocolate that interests them so much as it is the dollar bills tucked into the eggs.)

My Easter routine has always been the same. The night before the big hunt, I open sixty or more plastic eggs and stuff them with candy and money. I don't mind doing this job because nothing pleases me more than tearing open all of those candy bags and inhaling the rich, fragrant scent of chocolate. Once I've spread all the goodies across my bed to organize them by flavor and name brand, I'm like a drug addict set loose in a meth lab. I sample each candy before stuffing the rest into the eggs, and, as expected, I end up suffering the consequences of sugar overload and an unsettled stomach. Translation—quality time on the crapper.

The morning of Easter itself, I rouse my husband at the break of dawn to hide the plastic eggs in the backyard. If any of the kids have slept over at our house, my spouse takes sadistic pleasure in waking them by banging a wooden spoon against a metal frying pan. They emerge bleary-eyed from the dark caverns of their rooms and blink like moles in the blinding sunlight. I sit back with a steaming mug of coffee and watch while four grown children root around in the shrubs for the coveted, money-filled eggs. It never fails that every year one egg is lost, left to disintegrate in the grass until the following winter, when some fortunate soul will eventually stumble across a cracked egg with a damp, faded dollar bill inside.

Easter is all fun and games until the candy is gone and we find ourselves suffering serious sugar withdrawal for a week—not to mention the days spent picking little balls of discarded, colored foil out of the carpet and yanking strands of Easter grass out of the vacuum brushes.

Now that my kids are grown, I've turned my attention to my granddaughter, so she can experience the joy of an Easter egg hunt. I see years of chocolate bunnies in her future—and in mine.

The Birthday Party I Don't Remember

WE HAD PLANNED IT for months. It was to be the birthday party to end all birthday parties. The bar, disc jockey, and babysitter had all been reserved, along with a food and decorating committee. I'd even bought a beautiful, white silk pantsuit for the momentous occasion.

On the big day, my brother surprised me with a bottle of Dom Pérignon (nectar of the gods) and my husband had arranged for a brand new vehicle to be delivered to our home. It was the perfect day, but I don't do well with perfection. Somehow I always find a way to screw things up, and today was to be no exception.

Two hours before the party started, my husband was in the driveway signing papers with the car salesman. The cold bottle of Dom was calling my name from the refrigerator. I drank the first glass while I finished putting on my makeup. I drank the second (and third) while I was curling my hair.

By the time I was pouring my fourth glass, my husband had finished the deal and was handing me the keys to my new birthday present. At this point I feel I should mention that I didn't eat before the party. I'd been dieting for days so that I wouldn't look like a rotund polar bear in the white pantsuit. I was about to learn that champagne + empty stomach = TROUBLE.

By the time we arrived at the club, my nerves had kicked in at the prospect of hosting a party for seventy people. I needed another drink. I quickly marched up to the bar to place my order. The minute my mouth shouted "Sex on the Beach!" my brain silently protested the onslaught of more booze. Someone slipped the bartender a few extra bills to make the drink stronger for the birthday girl. Yeah, like I needed that.

I pinched my nose and chugged the drink to calm my nervous excitement. Oh, vodka, you fickle bitch, convincing women they can move like a pole dancer to any pulsating beat from a DJ's sound system. The siren song of alcohol soon warped my perception, allowing me to believe I was a sexy seductress in a snug white pantsuit. I sidled up to every male in the room (including the janitor and one skittish waiter) and latched onto each one like I was a she-wolf in heat. My husband was busy playing host and didn't seem to notice that his wife was quickly turning into a party train wreck.

That evening, twenty years ago, is still a blur to me. I have a vague recollection of stumbling through some horrid line dances and stepping on many toes. I know that I never got to blow out the candles or taste the birthday cake because I was too busy ralphing up Sex on the Beach in the toilet. My beautiful white pantsuit was turned into a Jackson Pollock painting with red cranberry juice splatters all down the front. The only thing I do vividly remember is my sister and my best friend holding my hair out of my face so that I wouldn't wake the next morning with puke-encrusted strands.

It took several men to carry me down a flight of stairs to the car, and believe me, this scene was nothing like Madonna's "Material Girl" music video. You know the one—where all the male dancers are carrying the sexy, writhing singer down the stairs? Oh, I was writhing all right. Writhing in agony because my stomach had not yet finished giving up the ghost.

I learned the next day that everyone at the party had happily carried on without me and (thankfully) no lap dances had been performed.

After I woke from my alcohol-induced coma with a headache that made me wish for a lobotomy, I crawled to the phone to start my long list of apologies to the guests. Moral of the story: tequila might make a woman's clothes fall off, but Dom makes me dumb and vodka makes me vampy. Next time, I'll wear camo to the party to hide the upchuck spatter.

The Do's and Don'ts of Valentine's Day Gifts

FOR WOMEN, VALENTINE'S DAY automatically conjures up images of candlelight dinners, gorgeous flowers, and decadent chocolates nestled in red satin hearts. Sadly, men have a completely different perspective of the holiday—one that involves obligation and a whole lot of pressure to get the right gift. I've seen plenty of men break into a sweat while checking out the card aisle at Hallmark. They know that if they screw this day up, instead of getting a roll in the hay, they'll end up in the dog house with Fido the Farter.

If a man's goal is to reach the Holy Grail of love before the champagne grows warm, he should follow this checklist of do's and don'ts for a successful Valentine's Day celebration:

- Don't buy the cheesy, stuffed bear in the convenience bin near the drugstore checkout line. Chances are your special lady has twenty more just like it in a garbage bag at the back of her closet. If she wants something cute and fuzzy, buy her a hamster.
- Nothing screams "last minute gift" more than three dozen wilted roses purchased for three dollars from a roadside stand. And don't steal flowers from your neighbor's garden in an effort to create a clever bouquet. A florist you are not. Whip out your skinny wallet and buy some REAL flowers that last more than a day.

- When it comes to chocolate, don't buy that cheap crap that leaves a waxy feel on the roof of her mouth. If the candies are covered in a white film, the box has most likely been sitting on the store shelf since Valentine's Day 2010. This is the one time you don't want to skimp on quality. Buy your woman some damn Godiva.
- Wine makes a perfect gift, unless it comes from the Swamp Gator Winery in the Florida Everglades. The same goes for champagne. If it looks like it was bottled in someone's carport, you might want to shell out some extra cash for the good stuff.
- Taking your significant other to Denny's for the one dollar and ninety-nine cent dinner special is NOT a romantic gesture. Take her to a restaurant that has more than three stars attached to its name. If Salisbury steak and pancakes are listed on the menu, and there's a chocolate dipping fountain in the center of the room, you're in the wrong place.
- Don't shop the local flea market for fake silver that looks like it came from a vending machine at a carnival. If you're going to be THAT cheap, the least you can do is throw in a bag of popcorn or roasted peanuts.
- When your woman hinted that tickets to a show might be nice, she wasn't referring to a Monster Jam where the 4x4s have tires the size of three-story donuts. Get her a dozen Krispy Kremes and take her to the movie theater.
- Thinking of shopping at Victoria's Secret for your love? Be very careful. If you buy her a thong two sizes too small, she'll obsess about her weight. If you buy her one in rhino-size that could double as a slingshot, you risk sleeping on the couch for a week.
- Caviar is a tricky gift. If it's beluga from the Caspian Sea, your partner will love it. If the container of caviar is marked "Made in Hong Kong," she might end up in the bathroom all night. Then the only action you'll see will be with a mop and a bottle of disinfectant.

Fellas, if you follow this checklist, you're sure to have a rewarding evening full of surprises—or maybe just a furry hamster.

Fifty Shades of a Renaissance Festival

IF YOU'VE NEVER BEEN to a Renaissance festival, you're missing out on the chance to travel back in time to the fifteenth century. Where else can you experience an archaic privy, a field of royal encampments, pirate raids, and stout for breakfast?

I'm a fourteen-year veteran of the Ren Fest, and a firm believer that everyone should, at least once in their lifetime, lace up their boots, tighten their corsets, and visit the local faire.

Attending a Renaissance festival allows you to experience the ultimate in role playing. Other than Halloween, this is the only time of year you can let your freak flag fly and put on a pirate hat, fairy wings, or a king's crown. There's no social hierarchy among the attendees of a Renaissance festival—CEOs dressed as saucy wenches rub elbows with middle school janitors in royal garb. No one cares about your net worth or your upbringing; the only things you'll be judged on are your swordsmanship and beer-drinking skills.

The food is a gastronomical dream. Turkey legs. Fried pickles. Chocolate-covered bacon on a stick. Did they have all of these delicacies during the Renaissance? No. Would they have wanted them? Heck, yeah!

There are also countless games, none of which require a controller or a Wi-Fi hotspot. The festival is a great place to test your skills in axe-throwing, archery, and jousting, but a word of warning: the chances of you winning any of these tournaments are slimmer than those of finding the Holy Grail under the tool shed in your back yard. If you're lucky, you might win the consolation prize—a faux armor shield that reads, "I RODE ON A UNICORN HORN AT THE FAIRE!"

Ever hear of Ren Porn? There's more exposed skin at the faire than you would ever find on a topless beach in Nice. Women wear gowns with necklines down to their navels and the men in tights leave little to the imagination. You'll see tattoos in places you never thought possible. The manly men in kilts will keep you guessing as to whether or not they're wearing a boulder brace or going commando under their plaid skirts.

Another great thing about the Renaissance festival is that you can drink and be merry all day long, and if you don't have the taste buds for warm mead in a wooden mug, don't worry. There are plenty of rum runners and frozen mojitos at the faire's pub. If these wicked libations had been available back in the 1400s, you can bet there would have been fewer wars and more napping.

What sets the Renaissance festival rides apart from your typical carnival rides is the lack of electricity. When you climb into a spinning barrel or onto a giant rocking horse, your ride is going to be powered by sheer muscle. In other words, when you board the swinging pirate ship, a burly man in tights will be in control of your mortality. (Avoid any ride named "The Hurlinator." This is especially important if you've consumed a large plate of sausage and peppers and washed it down with too many mugs of mead.)

Where else but the Renaissance festival can you find a parade of wenches, cardinals, and knights? It's people-watching at its finest. But beware—the costumes tend to alter the personalities of the people wearing them, especially if they've added rum floaters to a few of those frozen concoctions at the pub. Just steer clear of the man dressed as a polka-dotted caterpillar.

There is also an abundance of arts and crafts available, if you like unusual souvenirs that you'll never use again—items such as didgeridoos and horned Viking helmets. Do NOT take the didgeridoo to work to show your friends. Blowing into a large wooden instrument to replicate the sound of an injured buffalo is NOT conducive to a happy work atmosphere, unless you buy a pipe for everyone in the office so you can all break out into an impromptu didgeridoo concert during your lunch hour.

If you're looking for Disney-quality shows, you're in the wrong century. There is nothing G-rated about the festival's bawdy humor, musicals, or daredevil acts. But you WILL laugh hard enough that a quick trip to a privy might be necessary. And if you like men with long poles on horses, then the jousting show is for you.

You'll also feel like you've stepped into a world created by Harlequin. Nothing is more romantic than being surrounded by people dressed like characters from the cover of a bodice-ripping romance novel. Love is in the air, along with alcohol and revealing clothes. Welcome to *50 Shades of Renaissance Grey*.

At the end of the day, when you leave with a big bag of kettle corn tucked under your arm, you'll be thankful to return to your modern-day conveniences. Nothing beats air conditioning and indoor plumbing—except maybe a slow-roasted turkey leg.

Ladies' Restroom Etiquette 101

I'VE GONE TO THE BATHROOM in some strange places: swamps, mountain trails, and one roadside stop in Italy where the toilet was a hole in the ground and the toilet paper was strips of torn newspaper. Over the course of my vast bathroom experience, I've come to the conclusion that there's a misconception floating around about the fairer sex being the neater and cleaner sex. Anyone who's ever walked into a ladies' public restroom knows this is a myth. A sign stating, "BIOHAZARDOUS MATERIALS INSIDE" should be posted outside each and every facility.

My daughters both work in corporate offices, and we all agree that certain rules of bathroom etiquette need to be enforced in the workplace. No one wants to be the habitual office pooper, but sometimes you just have to make a bombing run. If you do happen to be the stinker in the stall, the next person in line will be accused of leaving the smell, especially if there's hang time to it. So do her a favor and throw her a couple of courtesy flushes, why don't you?

Every corporate office also has stall stalkers. These polite ladies sit quietly in a stall and wait for everyone to leave so they can uncork the results of last night's chicken wing binge fest. These women are also known for stalking secret stalls throughout their office buildings, and will do whatever they need to do to poop in peace. They'll take a five-minute elevator ride to the handicapped stall on the twenty-fifth floor, if they have to.

Public restrooms are the stuff that nightmares are made of. College taught me never to use a bar bathroom after 11:00 p.m., because inevitably someone is crying or puking in the stalls. Impromptu road trips from my youth also proved to be a lesson in courage when the only available bathrooms were at lone gas stations in the middle of Nowheresville. I'm pretty certain those pit stops were the inspiration behind many Stephen King novels.

On a recent family vacation, I lost count of the times I played musical bathroom stalls with my daughters at truck stops. Not knowing what lurked behind Door Number One, Two, or Three often forced us into games of "potty roulette." Most of the restrooms we visited smelled like a fisherman's wharf and had not seen a janitor's mop since VCRs were the cool, new technological gadgets. There often was enough hair left behind to knit a small sweater, and the sanitary product disposal boxes were filled to capacity with mummified tampons.

I understand a woman's need to squat like a sumo wrestler over the toilet bowl to avoid the germ-infested seat. But ladies, if you're going to spray like a cat marking her territory, be a sweetie and wipe the seatie. If you're there to do some serious business, do us all a favor and flush the toilet. I don't need to know that your last meal included red peppers.

Whether it's out of laziness or just plain forgetfulness, there are plenty of women out there who could benefit from a refresher course in Bathroom Manners 101. In the meantime, the next time my daughters and I hit the road, we'll be packing Public Restroom Survival Kits (complete with rubber gloves and industrial-size jugs of antibacterial soap). Hopefully, we'll be able to right the wrongs of women's bad bathroom habits—one toilet at a time.

Twelve Reasons Why She's Your Best Friend

WHEN MY BEST FRIEND moved away several years ago, I was crushed. We had been friends since the late 1980s, and we shared just about everything. We raised our children together and spent our weekends sharing backyard barbecues. Some of my happiest memories are of twilight hours in her kitchen, where we would cook side by side, swap recipes, and gossip over a bottle of chardonnay while the kids played outside.

What makes a best friend? The certain qualities we look for in our gal pals—loyalty, honesty, and trust—form the trifecta of friendship. Once that has been established, it's the little things that are the glue that holds the friendship together:

1. She doesn't tag you in unflattering pictures on Facebook and is happy to crop any photos that make your hips look too big.

2. She tells you if you need to pop a mint, clip your nose hairs, or pluck your unibrow. Got spinach in your teeth? She'll help you dig it out. She'll also tell you if your armpits smell and even let you borrow her roll-on deodorant.

3. She keeps up with you shot for shot at the bar and will never judge you for getting sloppy drunk or crying over the man who broke your heart. She'll also hold your hair out of your face while you pray to the porcelain god.

4. She tells you if your new jeans really do make your butt look big.

5. She has your back at parties and will warn you if the guy you're flirting with has "douchebag" written across his forehead. She'll also alert you to any exes prowling the room, and will go into "guard dog mode" if any of them dare to come near.

6. She accompanies you to awkward appointments like bikini waxes and pap smears.

7. She's being honest about your new haircut when she asks you if your stylist's name is Edward Scissorhands.

8. When you need to break your diet with snack cakes or a tub of cheese balls, she'll break her own diet, too, in solidarity. She knows that if she helps you eat the junk food, you won't feel as guilty.

9. She shares embarrassing stories of sexual mishaps in the bedroom that are on par with yours, which makes you feel a whole lot better about that time you let some gas slip during an intimate moment.

10. She never tells your husband how much you REALLY spent on that new dress.

11. Your period syncs up with hers, enabling the two of you to sympathize with one another when you flip the switch into bitch mode.

12. She accompanies you to public restrooms and doesn't care if you pee in front of her. If you don't make it to the toilet on time and have an accident in her car, she's okay with that, too.

Soaring With Eagles

WHENEVER I SEE A DRAWING of a bird, I think of my sister Cherie. She had a fascination with birds and an encyclopedic knowledge of every species. She worked at a wildlife center and fostered all types of injured birds, but she had a particular fondness for birds of prey. She took beautiful photographs of hawks, eagles, and owls, and sketched them every chance that she had. Her artistic skills were impressive, and whenever I studied her drawings, I felt more than just her admiration for these birds; I saw her desire to share their fierceness, beauty, strength, and freedom.

She is gone now, but like a phantom limb, I still feel her presence—an ache deep in my soul, hollowing me from the inside out.

When I close my eyes, I see her standing at the top of Beartooth Pass in Montana. She waits beside a vast meadow patchy with snow, a camera dangling from her hand as she gazes up at a cloudless sky in search of eagles. She turns to me, grins, and aims the camera. I try to smile but my eyes burn from the snow's glare. The light is blinding. My breath is shallow in the thin air, as if I'm breathing broken glass.

Her ashes now drift across that very same meadow. I remember smoothing the white hospital sheets over her still form and thinking of that snow.

I see her now in the hazy dreams of midnight where hundreds of photographs fan across the years, breathing life into memories of her that still linger here: horseback riding through the rugged mountains of Wyoming; tears shimmering in her eyes at the Wagner Opera; laughing at Pike's Place Public Market in Seattle with the sweet juice of Bing cherries on her lips; her radiant grin the first time she held her newborn son; the quiet reverence we shared in the butterfly garden while hummingbirds hovered above our heads; jumping in puddles up to our knees and knowing how silly we looked—two young women dancing in muddy water while a storm raged around us.

There were so many nights when I was young that she would steal me from sleep for a drive along the beach. I curled beside her and watched the stars race past the windows like silver glitter scattering across a black velvet sky. I always felt like she was racing against the moon. And I never knew why.

My sister had an eating disorder. She was killing herself slowly, and I didn't know how to stop her. No one did. She wore her loneliness and disappointment like a heavy winter cloak, and I stood by, helpless, as the light in her bright hazel eyes dimmed to gray. A storm was raging, but she was no longer dancing in its rain. Something had broken inside of her, leaving her heart cracked in too many places. She had become like the wounded birds she once cared for.

When the call came, I raced down darkened streets, saw the moon spin past my windshield, and wondered if she remembered its pale yellow face peering above the ocean's rim so long ago.

Cherie was already in the deep sleep of a coma when I arrived at the hospital. I touched her cool hand and felt her standing at the foot of the mountain. Monitors then screamed their flat line goodbye and I knew she had already taken flight like the eagles.

I drifted for hours, suspended between anger and guilt. The tiles on the hospital floor were cold against my cheek like snow, like the brisk air that had stung my face on the top of Beartooth Pass, where I knew she had gone.

I never said I was sorry. I stood at her funeral and delivered a eulogy to a crowd that needed to hear that she lived a beautiful and graceful life. But I was a hypocrite because I knew far better than that. She had been dying inside for years, and no one could save her.

An autopsy report claimed my sister died from pneumonia, with a heart that was three times its normal size, because of her obesity. I prefer to think her heart was large because she loved so much.

What I never said, never shared, was that the morning after she died, a red-tailed hawk circled my yard and alit in the pine branches above me. I looked into his dark, unwavering gaze and saw my sister watching over me.

Her ashes, now swirling over a snowy mountain top in Montana, will never settle. They'll twist inside my grieving heart until I feel the last breath of winter.

In Memory of Cheryl Sue Kester: February 7, 1953 – October 31, 2009

Old Bag

THE OTHER DAY while I was driving, I hit the brakes and my purse fell off the passenger seat, all of its contents landing upside down on the floor. With no time to tidy the mess up at a red light, I blindly stuffed everything back inside, appalled when my fingers brushed against something sticky. I hadn't bothered to organize my purse in a while, and had no idea what I'd just touched. I was actually frightened to find out.

Yes, I'm one of those women who drags the same old bag around year after year until the seams split or an uncapped pen leaks into the fabric. I'm the odd one at the party with a white tote bag draped over my shoulder in the middle of December. I should have a sign taped to my back with the warning: "BAD WITH PURSES!"

I hate buying new purses and have little interest in swapping them out for other bags of various sizes and colors. I've never understood women who are capable of managing several purses at one time, and I'm a bit envious of their ability to match their bags to their shade of toenail polish. Perhaps if I was the corporate type, I'd have enough purses and shoes to match all my color-coordinated outfits. But the truth is, I work from home, and there's really no need to purchase one bag to match my bathrobe and another to match my ensemble of ratty shorts and a T-shirt with a ketchup stain. "Excuse me, sir, does this purse come in the color of red splotches and sweat stains?"

I own a simple, utilitarian brown bag that is shapeless, functional, and large enough to stuff half of my house into. At any given time, there might even be a kid or two inside. My purse is one of those special organizer bags that has millions of separate compartments, like the squares in a shadow box. I'm convinced these bags were designed for women with Attention Deficit Disorder. I can pack all kinds of stupid stuff in my purse, like a half-eaten lollipop, a stale cheese stick, an unspooled roll of dental floss, and a stack of crumpled napkins from last month's garden club luncheon.

I'm slow to change, but I'll admit that when I'm forced to buy a new purse, I feel hopeful, like I've been given a second chance to organize my life and start all over again. It's almost as if the purse is a projection of who I am. New purse, new me. The old bag is tossed into my closet, the graveyard for all my mismatched, outdated purses: my baggy giraffe tote, a leopard-print handbag, a gold-sequined purse that has seen better times, and a tiny, black leather pouch that dates back to my college days, when all I needed was a driver's license and a tube of lipstick to score a free drink at the bar.

I've kept my cheetah-print purse the longest, despite the holes in the lining where unknown amounts of makeup and coins have disappeared. Animal-print bags used to be sexy. If I carried one around now, I'd look like an unfashionable, middle-aged woman lugging around a dead zebra. Why I ever wanted bags that resembled large, exotic animals, I'll never know. Thank God I wasn't keen on elephants.

Some people feel that a woman's purse is a reflection of her housekeeping skills. The opposite is true for me. I keep a fairly clean house, but the contents of my purse look like the aftermath of a tornado. The fact of the matter is, I get a little bit lazy when I know there will be no unexpected visitors knocking at the door of my purse.

If my purse could talk, it would tell you that I'm usually distracted while I'm carrying it around on my shoulder, and that I'm negligent about throwing anything away. This means that my purse ends up doubling as my personal trash can. My husband once ventured inside in search of an insurance card; moments later, he looked like a shell-shocked soldier returning from the battlefields.

I've already been amazed more times than I can count by the contents of my purse. Fishing around inside it right now, the first thing I encounter is a wine cork from a celebration I don't remember. There's also an empty bottle of aspirin, the spare key to a neighbor's house (she moved away four years ago), a shriveled panty-liner, one fuzzy antacid tablet, a cracked compact mirror, a handful of expired credit cards, a deflated tube of lip gloss, a flattened granola bar, and a receipt from Walt Disney World, dated 2007. Oh, and that sticky stuff at the bottom of my purse? A melted taffy bar from Halloween.

I have plenty of boring stuff in there, too—cosmetic bag, cell phone, hairbrush, wallet. My purse can hold anything, which is why I like it. I can stuff it full with a change of clothes, two water bottles, a towel, and enough food to last a week in the wilderness. I really don't get women who pay thousands of dollars on designer bags the size of a postage stamp; I'll keep my ugly, suitcase-size purse until it finally expires from neatness neglect. And then I'll buy another one just like it, which I promise will remain clean and organized—for at least the first month.

White-Water Rafting and Other Things I'll Never Do

I'VE NOTICED A GROWING trend of people my age scrambling to complete a "Bucket List" of things they hope to accomplish before they die.

"I'm going to climb Mount Kilimanjaro with nothing but a camera and a protein bar in my pocket!"

"I'm going to bungee jump off the Empire State Building on New Year's Eve!"

"I'm going to break the world's record by riding on Walt Disney World's Space Mountain for seven days straight, or until I come down with a permanent case of vertigo!"

No, thanks. I'm pretty content with all the things I've seen and done in my lifetime. I have a husband, four great kids, eight pets, an endless supply of chocolate biscotti, and some mediocre wine. What more could a girl ask for?

However, there is a thing called a "Reverse Bucket List" that I can easily fulfill. This list includes things that I hope NEVER to accomplish. Maybe I've become jaded with age, a bit cynical and crabby at times, but one thing is certain: I know what I DON'T want to do with the rest of my life. Whether it's out of fear or self-preservation, it doesn't matter. I have valid reasons for not wanting to do certain things, which absolutely justify my paranoid tendencies. Consequently, I will never:

Go White-Water Rafting. Flying down a rapid river in a rubber boat at breakneck speeds with my ass scraping over rocks is not my idea of fun.

Eat Weird Food. Escargot, caviar, and raw oysters? No, thanks. And certainly not frog legs. They're chewy, fishy, slimy, and I can't bear to think of all the amputee frogs out there bound to wheelchairs for the rest of their lives.

Take a Vacation on a Cruise Ship. I have one word for you: TITANIC.

Poke a Cobweb. Spiders are smart. They're never around when you mess with their webs, but in reality they're lurking close by, sizing you up, and figuring out just how much sticky thread they'll need to spin in order to wrap you up tighter than an Egyptian mummy.

Roller Blade. There's no way those little wheels are going to support my weight while I'm rolling down the pavement at 50 miles per hour. I can think of better ways to spend my time than in an emergency room with a fractured elbow and a hospital television broadcasting barely audible reruns of *The Simpsons*.

Drive on Major Interstates. This is South Florida. Everyone here drives like they're Mario Andretti, pumped up on amphetamines and late for weekly anger management therapy.

Kill Cockroaches. As gross as these bugs are, the stuff that comes out of them when you squish them is even more disgusting. I prefer to spray them with poison until they become a new breed known as "powdery albino cockroaches." There's also this little thing called karma. The last thing I want to do is return to this world as a bottom feeder, waiting to be snuffed out under the heel of someone's shoe.

Give Up Sugar. Are you serious? Anything worth eating has sugar in it.

Watch National Geographic Specials. Although these documentaries are educational, I'm not into watching Arctic wolves tear apart caribou, or jaguars tackling a baby zebra for a midday snack.

"Bucket List"? Getting through the day without crossing paths with a mob of vengeful cockroaches or being forced to eat frog legs is good enough for me. But I wouldn't mind sitting back with a glass of mediocre wine and watching some fool strap on a bungee cord for a courageous leap into the unknown.

Musings in the Shower

I REMEMBER THE DAYS when a long, hot shower was a rarity. With four small children running rampant through our house, I was a pro at doing my business in the bathroom and grabbing a quick shower in under five minutes—long before that obnoxious, purple dinosaur on TV finished singing the "I Love You" song to my mesmerized children. (And during those five minutes, I was consumed with worry that someone might attempt to cook a Styrofoam plate in the oven or do their best Picasso imitation on the dining room table with indelible markers and spaghetti sauce.)

Now that my kids are older, I have the freedom to enjoy a long, hot, uninterrupted shower—with plenty of time to contemplate life's little mysteries. During these interludes, my brain often hop-skips down the narrow lane between *Weirdsville* and *Fantasy Island*. Here's an example of how my menopausal mind-collage works while I'm showering:

"Damn, I need a tan. How did I get so pale? Someone's going to mistake me for a blobfish if I go to the beach. Oh, who am I kidding ... I never swim at the beach anymore. I prefer to sit by the water and drink wine. LOTS of wine, so I can forget why I no longer own a bathing suit."

"Which reminds me, I've been neglecting my lady bits lately. Time to trim the garden."

"What's up with my stomach? Why can't someone invent a home liposuction kit? I bet the nineteen-year-old could come up with something, if he took our garden hose and hooked it up to some sort of suctioning device."

"Sheesh! Whoever used the bathroom last should have lit a candle. Why does poop have to smell so bad? Why can't it smell like roses? Because everybody would go around sniffing each other's butts like dogs, that's why. Being called an "a-hole" would actually be a compliment."

"The dogs are barking ... is that the doorbell?"

"It IS the doorbell! Are you effing kidding me? It's *seven o'clock* in the morning! I'm not answering it."

"But what if it's Publisher's Clearing House and I'm missing out on my ten-million-dollar prize? I could always throw on a towel and go out there ... but if they saw me like this, they'd probably run screaming down the block, and I'd never get my check. Wait. What if it's that creepy new neighbor with all the cats? Or a robber checking to see if anyone is home? He could be sneaking in right now and I wouldn't even hear him. What if I pull back the shower curtain and he's standing there with a knife in his hand? Stop it, Marcia! You're not in the middle of an Alfred Hitchcock movie. Just think positive thoughts, like sunsets on the beach, margaritas, guacamole, nachos ... No, no, no! You're on a diet, remember?"

"Hmmm, my scalp itches. Wonder if it's this new shampoo. Wasn't the teenager scratching his head last night at the dinner table? Uh oh. Maybe it's lice. OH GOD, DO I HAVE LICE? No way. School's been out for weeks now. The kid has only been hanging out with a few of his friends—but he has been outdoors a lot lately. Do squirrels carry lice? They're too cute to get lice. I wish I had a squirrel for a pet. He could sit on my shoulder and eat peanuts. I'd name him Jujubee. Or Stanley."

"Hey, why are there so many soap curds in the drain? Does no one else in this house know how to clean out a shower? Oh crap, the water is getting cold. Time to get out. I wonder if there are any avocados in the fridge. I could really go for some guacamole."

And that is how the mind of a menopausal mother works. Now if you'll excuse me, I have to answer the door. There's a man outside with a fistful of balloons and a large cardboard check.

From Empty Nest to Full House

OUR YOUNGEST IS ONLY a year from graduating, and between school, work, and an active social life, he's seldom home. When we noticed he was around less, and in light of the fact that our three older children had left years ago, my husband and I jumped on the chance to enjoy a taste of freedom as "almost" empty nesters. I started to cook less, nap more, and spend unlimited time in the garden. There were also plenty of uninterrupted moments of intimacy that helped bring romance and spontaneity back into our lives. My husband and I were rediscovering each other after thirty years of marriage—suddenly it was 1984 all over again.

Until karma came knocking at the door.

My oldest daughter was offered a job transfer that gave her the opportunity to move back to our hometown. She accepted the transfer, and a month later she arrived on our steps with a toddler on her hip and a moving van in the driveway. The quiet serenity I'd grown accustomed to vanished before the first suitcase was even unpacked.

Gone are the days of sharing a leisurely cup of coffee over the morning news. My husband and I now sip our warm java while watching Chuggington, with our granddaughter sandwiched between us on the couch.

And the changes haven't stopped there.

The living room that I used to keep as clean as a showroom floor is now littered with stuffed animals, a toddler trampoline, a plastic princess slide, and a talking choo-choo train. I have regular flashbacks to the days when I had four young children with enough toys and play equipment to run a small amusement park. I feel like I'm trapped in the Land of the Wee People, with all of the tiny little tables, tiny little chairs, and tiny little toys cluttering my home.

My life has become one long instance of *déjà vu* as I stress about spilled apple juice, gooey tabletops, and curious dogs choking on Lego blocks. There are condensation rings in the shape of the Olympics symbol on my fine wood furniture and mysterious stains on my couch that resemble a Rorschach ink blot test. These mishaps are a sharp reminder of the twenty years I spent with a roll of paper towels in one hand and a bottle of spray cleaner in the other.

I've learned that 8:00 p.m. is the witching hour for small children. The dreaded word "bedtime" automatically sets off a siren that can be heard six blocks away. It's the battle cry of every rebellious toddler waging a war against sleep. My granddaughter is no exception, and the high decibels of her nightly tantrums can make my ears bleed. Her shrieks set the dogs on edge, and within minutes my home sounds like it has been overrun by a pack of howling coyotes.

Extra people in the house also means that my garbage bin looks like Mount Trashmore, the laundry pile is the height of the Matterhorn, and the dirty dishes in the sink are stacked higher than Mount Fiji. My home has been transformed into a revolting mountain range.

I also deal constantly with unpleasant odors permeating the air, and I'm never quite sure if the smell is from a gassy pug or a diaper gone wrong. Pretty soon I'll need to invest in a Gag-O-Meter to determine the culprit behind each stink.

Other changes include a second refrigerator in our spare bedroom for our daughter's organic groceries. She prefers clean eating. The irony of this is not lost on me since all my children lived by the five second rule whenever food fell on the floor.

The extra stress from all the changes in our home has caused my husband to gnash his teeth down to the size of corn niblets, and just yesterday I noticed that my own night guard is now sporting new holes.

I may be on the verge of a middle-age meltdown, but in all the chaos, I've found magic. It comes in the form of a little girl's laughter when she rushes into my arms after her morning waffles, and plants a sticky kiss on my cheek. It's there, at the kitchen table, when I share a glass of wine with my daughter and we giggle and gossip into the wee hours of the night. More importantly, there's magic behind every "I love you," and in every embrace.

I miss the freedom of an empty nest, but I'll gladly trade it for a house full of laughter, and all the sticky kisses my granddaughter has to offer.

Acknowledgments

I'd like to thank my mother, Fay Kester, for the countless hours she spent editing my stories, and for the love and encouragement she provided daily when I was ready to quit. Her unwavering faith in me pushed me to work harder and to believe that nothing is impossible. "Look, Mum! Dreams really do come true!"

I'd also like to thank my dear friend Crystal Ponti for turning my vision into a reality. Her brilliance brought this book to fruition, and for that I will be eternally grateful.

A huge thank you to my editor, Sarah del Rio, for taking my vision to the next level. You waved your editing wand and created magic with this book. Thank you from the bottom of my heart for your time and effort.

Many thanks also go out to my wonderful team at Booktrope—Pam Labbe, Andie Gibson, and Michelle Fairbanks. Your creative collaboration has taken this book above and beyond my expectations. If you're ever in sunny south Florida, plan on dinner in my lovely backyard garden (along with unlimited rounds of frozen margaritas).

Special thanks to my four children—Jared, Jennifer, Jane, and Jack—for providing the hilarity that is our family life. You've brought so much love and laughter into my world, and have given me the reason to write this book—to keep the memories alive, one page at a time. I love you to the moon and back.

About the Author

Marcia Kester Doyle is the voice behind the popular humor blog Menopausal Mother, where she muses on the good, the bad, and the ugly side of midlife mayhem. Give her a glass of wine and a jar of Nutella, and she'll be your best friend.

Marcia has written for The Huffington Post, Humor Outcasts, In the Powder Room, and What The Flicka. Marcia has also been featured on numerous sites such as Scary Mommy, BlogHer, BonBon Break, Club Mid, Boomer Cafe, Vibrant Nation, The Erma Bombeck Writer's Workshop, Midlife Boulevard, Boomeon, and BA50, among others. She has contributed to the following books: *The Mother of All Meltdowns, Clash of the Couples, Motherhood: May Cause Drowsiness, Sunshine After the Storm, To Bliss and Back, Parenting Gag Reel, Surviving Mental Illness Through Humor* and *Mom for the Holidays,* and will be featured in the forthcoming anthology *How Can You Laugh at a Time Like This?*

Marcia is a BlogHer Voice of the Year 2014 recipient and VoiceBoks Top Hilarious Parent Blogger 2014. She was also voted as a Top 25 Blogger in the Circle of Moms Contest 2013. She is a native Floridian and married mother of four children, as well as being a grandparent to a feisty toddler.

Connect with Marcia

Humor Blog: www.menopausalmom.com
Facebook: www.facebook.com/MenopausalMother
Twitter: www.twitter.com/MenoMother
Instagram: www.instagram.com/marciakesterdoyle
Pinterest: www.pinterest.com/marciakdoyle
Official author website: www.marciakesterdoyle.com

MORE GREAT READS
FROM MILL PARK PUBLISHING

Midlife Cabernet by **Elaine Ambrose** won the Silver Medal for Humor from Indepdnent Publisher Book Awards, a 4-star review from ForeWord, and Publishers Weekly reviewed the book as "laugh-out-loud funny!" The book ranked #1 in humor sales on Amazon. Here's proof that there is life, love, and laughter after fifty.

Who Left the Cork Out of My Lunch? by **Vikki Claflin** is chock-full of funny, informative how-to lists, hilarious advice columns, and sharp personal anecdotes about menopause, empty nests, midlife sex, marriage, age-appropriate fashion, cosmetic intervention, beauty tips, and diets. An Amazon #1 best-seller, it's the How-To Guide for letting go of our youth and start rocking our middle age.

I Was in Love with a Short Man Once by **Kimberly J. Dalferes** (Humor) A book best read while wearing fuzzy bunny slippers. Both a bathroom and a beach read, you'll come to fully appreciate that there's always room for Jello, and tequila, and a funny book.

Magic Fishing Panties by **Kimberly J. Dalferes** (Humor) A book that reminds all women of certain truths: the best pals are gal pals; all anyone needs to rule the world is a pair of black boots and a fabulous red coat; and above all else, live out loud, laugh often, and "occasionally" drink tequila.

CPSIA information can be obtained
at www.ICGtesting.com
Printed in the USA
LVOW12s1937270717
542877LV00001B/27/P